VIRGIN

Meditations on History, Ecology, and Culture

FOREST

Eric Zencey

The University of Georgia Press

Athens and London

Published by the University of Georgia Press
Athens, Georgia 30602
© 1998 by Eric Zencey
All rights reserved
Designed by Erin Kirk New
Set in 10 on 13 Berkeley Oldstyle Medium by G & S Typesetters
Printed and bound by Maple-Vail Book Manufacturing Group
The paper in this book meets the guidelines for
permanence and durability of the Committee on
Production Guidelines for Book Longevity of the
Council on Library Resources.

Printed in the United States of America
02 01 00 99 98 C 5 4 3 2 1

Library of Congress Cataloging in Publication Data
Zencey, Eric, 1953–
Virgin forest : meditations on history, ecology, and culture /
Eric Zencey.
p.   cm.
These essays were written between 1985 and 1995; some essays
were published separately.
ISBN 0-8203-1989-9 (alk. paper)
1. Human ecology—Philosophy.   2. Philosophy of nature.
3. History—Philosophy.   I. Title.
GF21.Z46   1998
304.2—dc21   97-39240

British Library Cataloging in Publication Data available

For David Ingersoll,

Frank Kalinowski,

and John Rodman

Contents

Preface

The work collected here was written between 1985 and 1995, a period in which I taught, started a family, and otherwise built a life in Central Vermont. Many of these pieces were published separately during that time, but to think of what follows as a collection of separate essays tends, I think, to misrepresent it. Much as a fiction writer might produce something halfway between a novel and a collection of short stories by writing a series of related stories with a single group of characters who change and grow and move through the work as a whole, I wrote most of what's here with the work's cumulative effect in mind. Or, to be absolutely accurate: after publishing "Apocalypse and Ecology" and "Some Brief Speculations on the Popularity of Entropy as Metaphor" in the *North American Review,* I began to shape the nonfiction I wrote to join those pieces in forming a single volume, one dedicated to exploring the related problems of history and nature in industrial culture. I conceived of it as forming one extended essay—an essay by turns narrative and argumentative, philosophical and autobiographical, historical and personal.

Each of the essays in this volume deals in its way with a central problem: how are we to conceive of our relationship to nature now that we can no longer convincingly pretend that nature is something separate and distinct from culture, infinitely exploitable and infinitely tractable? How can we make ourselves a place—politically, morally, practically—in the world as it is, a world suffering the ecological and temporal dislocations of modernity, a world in which civilization threatens its own material roots in nature? How can we be truly at home in such a world, in post-Nature nature? What will ground us? What will guide us?

The answer I've come to is "history."

Over time I've come to realize that our ecological crisis is also a historical crisis. By this I mean not that the moral and ecological problems that result from our technological, industrial domination of nature have become manifest at a particular historical moment (although, of course, they have) or that our ecological problems are serious enough that they have to be mentioned in any narrative account of our culture that tries to be complete (although I believe they are). What I mean is this: the cultural attitudes toward nature that produced our ecological crisis have symptomatic and consequent parallels in our cultural attitudes toward history. If we are out of place in nature, we are also out of place in time, and the two kinds of exile are related.

As exiles we seem to have nothing to give us moral grounding but our own say-so, and we don't like that feeling of floating free, self-contained and weightless, in space. But what are the alternatives? Commandments from on high are out. God is either dead, or departed, or speaking to us privately rather than civically, or (thanks to our commendable toleration of diversity) speaking to us in such a cacophony of voices that He or She no longer offers much that can be turned to general civic use. Tradition won't do: much cultural practice is demonstrably wrongheaded, and to pick only what we like undercuts the one quality that lets tradition serve as a moral ground, its semblance of impersonal, inevitable necessity. Science is complicit in the domination of nature (although, to be fair, it also helped us recognize its own faults here), and its usefulness to the task of building an objective, legitimate-because-in-some-sense-"true" moral vision has been undercut by relativism and revisionist criticism, movements that challenge the very existence of truth and that reveal just how often we've taken *objective* to mean "that which is in the interests of the powerful."

In the past we turned to Nature, which stood outside culture, far enough at least that it could be represented as a source of the kind of transcendent and regulatory value we need. It offered a ready supply of ideas, images, and metaphors that weren't obviously human in origin. Darwin's nature with its struggle for survival supported Adam Smith's Invisible Hand; the Great Chain of Being supported a political system with a rigid hierarchy of class; the idea of the Noble Savage supported romanticism's dissent from industrial culture; and more recently ecology has been enlisted to support an image of political community as Egalitarian, Nonhierarchical Web. But Nature is now "Nature"—it has those postmodern quotation marks around it to show that we know it's a social construct. Darwin read Thomas Malthus, not the other way around. Whatever lessons for political organization or moral life we extract from nature usually turn out to be ones we projected there in the first place.

Still, I believe it's possible to derive regulatory moral value from nature historically understood. Over time nature reveals to us fairly unambiguously what is and isn't wise for us to do if we are to live in harmony with it. And even if the cultural wisdom we need about life in harmony with natural systems is slow to form in our collective awareness, there is an additional reason to cultivate a historical understanding: the judicious pursuit of such understanding is crucial to a moral life.

Why this is so emerges, I hope, from the work that follows.

No book is the product of a single mind. Because this book is in part the record of how I have grappled with these questions in my life, and because no single *life* is the product of a single mind, either, my duty of acknowledgment is all the greater. By rights I should thank not just the people who read various parts of the manuscript but every person who contributed to the ideas, experiences, and understandings the book recounts. (Can the impossible ever be morally obligatory?) But even if it were possible, a comprehensive list would test the patience that every author of a preface assumes from a willing readership. Let me say, sweepingly, that my thanks go to a decade's worth of students and colleagues and college-cafeteria-table interlocutors, to friends old and new, to dinner companions and conference compatriots, and to a handful of journal editors, all of whom helped me clarify my thinking (and my prose) by letting me know what they thought.

After waving an arm so broadly, let me point more specifically: the dedication acknowledges the three most influential teachers I've had. Their presence can be felt on every page.

Acknowledgment of help received during such long-gestating work necessarily tests the memory—another spur to sweeping, general-category thanksgiving. But even with all bases lightly swept, some people need to be mentioned who read or heard parts of the manuscript or listened to the ideas behind it and offered useful, instructive response: Alexandra Altman, Tim Brookes, Brigid Clark, David Colander, Deb Crespin, Mark Doty, Judy Francis, Paul Garstki, Louise Glück, Carrie Grabo, Wil Hamlin, Lois Harris, Jack Kytle, Frank Lambert, Syd Lea, Deborah Maine, Todd Maitland, Joanna Meyer, Benjamin Neilson, John Schaar, Deborah Schupack, Gus Seelig, Elaine Segal, Tracy Strong, Bill Vander Clute, Bill Vitek, and Beverly T. Wiebe. Chris Noël read each piece as it was written as well as the manuscript as a whole and offered invaluable assistance in both stages. Of course, the responsibility for such errors of fact, judgment, taste, dogma, or design as the work still contains is mine alone.

To Robley Wilson Jr., editor of the *North American Review,* I owe a debt of gratitude; his free rein and gentle blue pen were just what I needed. To my editor at the University of Georgia Press, Barbara Ras, whose confidence in the value of this project was a source of encouragement for the three or four years we had it under discussion, I owe much thanks—not only for that encouragement but also for concrete suggestions that made the work stronger. Many thanks go as well to Leslie Daniels and to my agent, Joy Harris, whose work with another project helped create the room in my life for finishing this one.

To Kathryn Davis I owe a debt that can't be paid. Without her confidence, her ideas, her keen comprehension, and especially without her shaping hand and fiction writer's eye this work would not exist—or, existing, would have been a meager thing and poorly formed at that.

The following works were originally published in slightly different form in the *North American Review:* "Apocalypse and Ecology" (summer 1988); "Some Brief Speculations on the Popularity of Entropy as Metaphor" (fall 1986); "On Hunting" (summer 1987); "Cartography" (summer 1989); "The Contemporary Relevance of Henry Adams" (October 1991); "The Hand That Wounds" (summer 1990); and "In Search of Virgin Forest" (September 1993). "The Rootless Professors" was first published in the *Chronicle of Higher Education* (June 1985) and was reprinted in *Rooted in the Land: Essays on Community and Place,* edited by William Vitek and Wes Jackson (New Haven: Yale University Press, 1996). "Why History Is Sublime" was published in January 1989 in the now defunct *North by Northeast.* A portion of "Zeno's Mall" appeared in the April 1997 *Hungry Mind Review,* an issue dedicated to the Mall of America. "Ecology and Guilt" was written for presentation at the Southwest Social Science Association's annual meeting in March 1994.

Virgin Forest

Apocalypse and Ecology

On the evening of October 22, 1844, a quiet and selective exodus took place in New England. Fifty thousand citizens left their homes as though for the last time, pulled out-of-doors and away from their neighbors as smoothly as a sharper's hand draws an ace from a deck of cards. Here an entire family left their farm, its fields tangled by a summer of neglect; there, in a small town, a wheelwright or a cooper or a smith marshaled his children and wife out of the house, gave a moment's pause at the bolt, then left the door ajar. No doubt in some homes only a few felt the impulse. We can imagine an elder son pausing at the door, wearing the sort of rude gown all fifty thousand had been directed to sew in preparation, his purpose delayed for a moment by pity for those he could not convince. Then he moved on to join the others, the believers who gathered on a hilltop outside of town.

On dozens of hilltops they waited, their gowns pale and thin against the starry autumn night. They looked to the heavens; perhaps they talked quietly. Around them their children may have played or stood, sullen, subdued by the compulsion of reverence, the attraction of sleep. The sky was clear, not yet obscured by the cold front that would move in from the Midwest before morning, bringing with it lowering clouds and an unfulfilled promise of drizzle. Finally to be doing the thing that had been predicted, the thing they had waited for, the thing that had given their days on earth their meaning: together now, among their own and away from the puzzled, critical eyes of neighbors and kin, their relief must have been palpable.

All across New England, fifty thousand people waited until morning for the advent of Christ.

I'm not interested so much in the compulsion that led these fifty thousand to leave their worldly possessions, dress in ritually simple cloth, and sit on mountains. (That, as a matter of historical record, had to do with the teachings of one William Miller, a Baptist preacher-farmer, whose careful study of the Bible led him to conclude, in 1818, that the world would end in 1844.) I am interested in how these faithful must have felt on the morning of October 23, when the dawn came with its ordinary beauty. How, I want to know, did any of them find their way back down their mountain?

I suspect I know the answer. Although my mountain top was not as literal as those climbed by the Millerites that evening, I climbed it twenty years ago in the same spirit of certainty, anticipation, and hope. I was no Millerite. I had learned ecology.

To many of us who accepted the teachings of ecology history had a particular form. There was the recent past, the three or four thousand years of civilization, a period whose record revealed beyond doubt a pattern of human abuse of nature and offered to the wary observer clear grounds for predicting its inevitable result. Beyond the recent past, in the shadowy world of prehistory, was a state of ecological grace: hunters and gatherers living in harmony with nature, grouped in nomadic tribes with a preliterate but rich and participatory culture, whose numbers and practices never exceeded the planet's capacity to support and adapt to them. And in the future . . . in the future there was discontinuity, a dramatic change, a momentous upheaval, out of which would come new practices and a new society wise to the lessons of ecology.

The message was hard to avoid. In Geology 105, along with four hundred other underclassmen in the darkened lecture hall, I saw slides showing how long the world's known petroleum reserves would last at present rates of consumption. The bell-shaped curve was thin and pinched, with a horrendous peak in the mid-seventies and then a precipitous decline to the year 2000. (In the bright lecture hall of Economics 105 the professor tried to reassure us we would never run out of oil: the last barrel would be too expensive to use and would probably be bought at auction for display in a museum. By then, he told us, the market would have discovered alternatives. Economics, under pressure, had abandoned the myth of infinite resources and regrouped behind the myth of infinite substitutability. Geology was more intimately acquainted with physics and the truths of thermodynamics.)

And then a number of us turned an upper-division seminar in world politics into a court of inquiry into the probable future of the technological-industrial world order. The putative subject was American security policy, but the professor gave us free rein, so long as we nodded in the direction of geopolitics when introducing arguments about resource scarcity. Should America be dependent on foreign oil? We delighted in the paradoxes, the ironies, to which this question led. Yes, we could answer, if we want to give Middle Eastern sultans and madmen the power to choke our economy to death. No, we could answer, if we want to ensure that after a few decades of vigorous pumping of its domestic reserves America will be helplessly dependent on foreigners for its oil.

Such paradoxes delight only if you have an intimation of their transcendence, and we did. In the radical reaches of the environmental movement there was a vision, grounded in ecology, of how things might be if humans did not dominate nature. Compounded out of the works of Paul Shepard, E. F. Schumacher, Murray Bookchin, Barry Commoner, Amory Lovins, and others, this vision gave us comfort and guided our approach to the history of political philosophy. The issue was simple: Would America succumb to technological fascism, or would our freedoms be preserved the only way they could—through a radical decentralization of political power and an equally radical economic transformation, a revolution to reverse the Industrial Revolution itself, one that would eliminate all but sustainable enterprises using renewable fuels and minimizing resource use?

We were optimists, filled with confidence in the power of education, and so the first course didn't seem likely. Oh, we suspected that in the short run resource scarcity and a declining standard of living would prompt our country into imperial aggression and domestic repression. But we knew that this course depended on both a rapacious use of resources and a companion faith in the ability of technology to solve the problems that technological domination of nature creates, and the smart money was betting against both. Reason, we thought, would prevail. The earth is finite, and because of that there are limits both to the resources we can appropriate and to the ability of ecosystems to absorb our increasingly toxic garbage. As we approached those limits the lesson would become obvious. Just about everyone would see that we would have to change our ways. And so we were secure in our belief in the coming transcendence of industrial society.

This view had much to commend it and still does, though I think now that we underestimated the ability of high industrial culture to muddle along, disguising its centralizing, technocratic tendencies with the trappings of mass democracy and forcing its most unpleasant ecological consequences on subject peoples far, far from the routine purview of American voters. I have also come to suspect that the end point of this belief—a faith in the apocalyptic transformation of industrial culture—is no different in kind from the faith that moved the Millerites to the tops of their mountains.

There is a seduction in apocalyptic thinking. If one lives in the Last Days, one's actions, one's very life takes on historical meaning—and no small measure of poignance. But along with that historic importance can come a kind of paralysis. My belief made it difficult for me to do anything that required planning very far in advance, for I could not conceive of a future that was an organic outgrowth of my moving present. On the calendar I kept in my head the days and weeks were a grid of rolling, checkerboard fields, and the farthest horizon I could imagine was only a year or two away.

Partly this marks a natural limitation of youth, of course, but my generation was encouraged to make of youth a moral claim: we sixties-era baby boomers would show our solidarity with oppressed peoples everywhere and with the earth itself by refusing to let the inertia of cultural custom be manifest within us. We would refuse to imagine a future continuous with our present.

Thus, unwittingly, did we accept the condition that would best guarantee our own estrangement.

I began to change my way of thinking when my daughter was born, when I began to appreciate the value of having insurance, a form of security forbidden by the dictatorship of spontaneity. Somewhere in the back of my mind had been a deeply buried belief that I would never need insurance, not because I hadn't faced the certainty of my own mortality but because I knew that *things wouldn't go on like this forever.*

I'm not sure what I envisioned. It was hard to see exact details of the social order across the general chaos that would come as the radical transformation of everything existing. I just knew that whatever happened—generalized commune life, a return to small town values and society, a poster-perfect realization of face-to-face democracy and an absence of industrial anonymity—my future would be assured, and I didn't need insurance. I belonged to a new tribe, and the tribe would care for me, just as I was caring for it by picking up every hitchhiker I saw and offering the hospitality of my home and larder to every casually introduced, non-surnamed stranger who came my way.

With the birth of my daughter there came upon me a growing sense that life endures and a realization that my own life was actually happening, not being held in suspension until the day that my beliefs would be vindicated by event. There grew within me a suspicion that *life might go on like this forever.* Hadn't my parents, whose ideas were settled on them in the long dark age before Hiroshima and Earth Day One, suffered through some of the same anxieties, the same whining tantrums, the same panic on the way to the doctor's for stitches? I began projecting myself ahead ten, twenty, thirty years. What would it be like when my daughter left for college? What sort of old person would I be? I joined the retirement program at work. I drove my wife crazy. Do you think, I asked her one quiet summer afternoon as we sat sunning ourselves and reading in the yard, miles away from any other people, that we'll be able to get up out of these chairs when we're sixty? She said the question depressed her. I don't think she appreciated what was behind it. I was reimagining myself in time; I was finding my way across a wound in history.

I never felt as though it were a wound *I* had made. And although my acceptance of it is what made it real for me, I hadn't made that wound alone. Our culture encourages a pathological denial of the continuity of history. A full account of the sources of this pathology would have to mention our nation's mythology of self-creation, by which we tell ourselves that the United States, alone among nations, was able to break the corrupting hold of tradition upon institutional structure; our relative youth as a nation, which gives us a landscape devoid of the object lessons to be found in the ruins and architectural leavings of progenitor civilizations; the fact that we are a mobile society, disconnected from place and hence from an objective correlative for any sense of the continuity of time through history; and also our industrial development and population growth, which continue to transform the landscapes we inhabit, reinforcing the notion that nothing is permanent, leading even fifteen-year-olds to express nostalgia for the world of their youth.

And there are other, broader forces at work. Economics, which has emerged as the queen of our social sciences, is profoundly ahistorical—not just in the sense that it mirrors and supports the industrial culture that it explains, complete with its spurs to immediate gratification (in which the future is discounted as being distant and somehow less real) and its consummate faith in the ideology of progress (in which the past is rendered irrelevant, because inferior), but also because in theory and in practice economics assumes that nature itself is ahistorical. Economists, that is, explicitly assume that the environment in which economic activity takes place is not affected by that activity but is instead permanent and unchanging—an essence that exists separate from us, outside our temporally bound culture. Finally, and perhaps most subtly, ours is still largely a Judeo-Christian culture, and from that tribe of wanderers who retreated from the hard facts of Roman occupation into the never-never land of religious apocalypse we inherited not only our sense of the shape of history—innocence, then the fall, then apocalyptic redemption—but also the legacy of resentment that longs for revenge through a final, accounts-balancing judgment of those who do us wrong.

When did history break? We might, for convenience's sake, select 1939 as the year of rupture, the year the General Electric Corporation invented the term *time capsule* for the cylinder they sponsored at the New York World's Fair, in which was placed, among other items, a ten-million-word essay describing contemporary civilization, a copy of the Bible, reproductions of works by Picasso and Grant Wood, and the Lord's Prayer translated into three hundred languages. Certainly in the urge to arrange artifacts for future discovery we can sense an anxiety about the discontinuity of history, even as the action itself affirms a faith that there will be a future, complete with humans interested in some form of archaeology. We might go back further: to the clear-sighted eyes of Henry Adams, the 1890s offered ample demonstration that the narrative thread of the world had been broken, that all and everywhere was gibberish, cacophony, decline. Or we might take our symbolic year to be 1945, the year we humans were first forced to confront the possibility of an apocalyptic end suffered at our own hands. A good case can be made for the symbolic importance of a later date, sometime in the mid-1980s (the exact year is difficult to determine from census figures), when, for the first time, a majority of adult Americans had been born *since* 1945.

With that demographic development, as predictable and as foreseeable in its way as the encroachment of the Ice Age glaciers, came a subtle change in America's political psyche, a change that is difficult to spy directly, difficult to map and explore. We still experience cyclic swings between cynicism and hope, between public generosity and Social Darwinism, between isolation and empire, between a politics of moral principle and a politics of greed and resentment. But the very groundwork of our politics has changed, slowly reflecting the increasing presence in our polity of individuals who have known all their lives that at least one of the dark corners of our future is illuminated by an artificial sun, a sudden and brilliant light that will be followed by darkness, silence, and the end of human history.

There are times when, skiing up the hill to the southeast of my house on a winter afternoon, I find the windows lit with a red and intensified reflection of the sunset. The first time I saw it—year two of the presidency of Ronald Reagan, that actor who once affably joked into an open mike, "Today I signed legislation declaring the Soviet Union illegal. The bombing starts in five minutes"—I had an instant of uncontrolled panic: *Oh, my god. Plattsburg! They've taken out the air base.* This is the way that images of nuclear holocaust intrude themselves into our consciousness—by accident, by surprise, by an epileptic short-circuiting of the defenses we construct, like a barricade against a door, out of the heavy furniture of routine. I quickly recovered my composure, my "rational" apperception. But I was left with a sense of the profound unfairness of such an apocalypse—there would be no discrimination between the guilty and innocent, no sorting of saved and damned; how could they!—and an unshakable feeling that I was powerless to make effective the answer I want to give to the question that is always implicitly before us, a question that previous cultures never had to face: Shall there be a future, or not?

   After the birth of my daughter, the image of nuclear destruction no longer weighed down my thoughts as often as it used to. I know that for other parents the reaction is different. Having children makes them feel more keenly the threats that pose a hazard to the life they've created, and they're more likely to take history personally, to see it not as a distant process that wears upon anonymous strangers but as the habitat of self, of the self's own flesh and blood. While my daughter's birth encouraged me to take history personally, I found that my ambition to affect the world was diminished after her birth, as if my notion of public obligation and my faith in the apocalypse were ready to be discarded. It could be that my apocalypticism was rooted in a narcissistic urge to be important and that becoming a parent fulfilled that pathetic desire. Certainly my child depends on me as no one ever has, and I have on occasion found solace in knowing that she would lift me out of anonymity, that in her memory I could not be one among the faceless many who populate the earth and leave no record. And perhaps in the routines of parenthood I have found additional weight to throw against the door that holds back an all-too-rational fear of a nuclear end to all things, the fear that encouraged me to accept a more optimistic mythology of apocalypse.

Perhaps. But I think there was something else going on as well. Apocalypticism fulfills a desire to escape the flow of real and ordinary time, to escape the flow of history by fixing it into a single moment of overwhelming importance. But from the moment my daughter was born I knew she would most assuredly grow up in real time, and I began to realize that I would miss out on something were I to hold myself aloof from her life by dismissing it, out of hand, as happening Before the Apocalypse.

It is ironic that the ecology movement, in offering a vision of a sustainable society, drew some part of its strength from a mentality that was, by its very nature, not sustainable. Movements that accept such a contradiction between ends and means—movements that say, in effect, "We will do this until such time as victory is assured, and then we will change"—have not generally accomplished their aims. Certainly the ecology movement would have done better—and would do better in the future—if its partisans had drawn their image of time not from the romantic notion of history, with its

apocalyptic redemption, but from nature, where there is no apocalypse, just continual (and sometimes admittedly dramatic) adaptation and change.

I still believe that industrial culture is not sustainable and that
therefore it will, in time, change, and change drastically. But the
scale of time in which that change will happen is most likely to be
larger and longer than an individual human life. There won't be a
particular morning on which we rise and stretch and, glancing out
the window, realize that it has happened. The rhythm of the apocalypse will be in geologic time, where a crisis can last a thousand
years and the moment of judgment—if indeed it is fair to use that
word to describe a natural process—can be played out in centuries.

Humans cannot inhabit geologic time, but they can and do imagine it and use it as a conceptual lens, as one among many ways to
conceive of time. None is necessarily better than another—the geologic time scale is not absolutely better than my graduate school
checkerboard field as a framework for temporal organization. The
worth of any one way of thinking about time depends, pragmati-
cally, on the matter at hand. To fix on any single image to the exclu-
sion of others is to deny ourselves some part of the richness of human experience, in which our moving present has the potential to
be woven from any of the threads of the densely textured temporality of our world. The richest life, it seems to me, is lived in an
awareness of the maximum number of connections backwards and
forwards in time, all of which are brought together in the individual's experience of the narrow moment of "now." Apocalypticism
is a pathological breaking of the continuity of time. When we are
under its spell, we cannot integrate what we know of the past and
what we imagine of the future into a rich, complex present.

And so I find myself drawn to the study of history in a way I never
was twenty years ago, when all I wanted was to understand how we
had come to be suspended on the edge of apocalypse. As I drive
down winding, two-lane Route 14 on my way to work, I find myself
trying to imagine how the valley I traverse would have looked to its
residents a hundred years ago. What I want to understand clearly

is how it is the same and how it is different. Here and there I can see where the old wagon road used to go. I can gauge the relative newness of the paved road from the way the fill has altered the course of the North Branch, which runs along it. Downstream from LeClerc's horse field, where the road cuts a corner and forces the stream into a right-angle turn, the meanders are migrating, testifying to the disturbance. They now work their way into hillsides they must have long ago reconciled themselves to.

When I take Route 2 east along the Winooski River, toward New Hampshire, I follow the East Branch into Marshfield. Local legend has it that long ago, on top of one of the hills that surround the town, a group of people gathered to await the end of the world. Once I asked at the Marshfield General Store if they had been Millerites. "Goodness, I don't know," the old woman behind the counter replied. "They were a little crazy," she added.

No doubt Millerites everywhere were disappointed by the failure of Christ to show at the appointed time. Some, disillusioned, left the church. But a surprising majority came to accept the explanation that on October 22, 1844, Christ *began* his final judgment, a lengthy process that continues today. These faithful, unshaken, helped transform the Millerite cult into an accepted denomination. They invented an institution, an appropriate bureaucracy, and a manner of sustainable routine commensurate with their vision. To do so they had to discard the image of time they had once eagerly embraced. Like those ancient adventurers who, upon returning home, discovered that they could hardly understand the gestures and accents of people who once had been their neighbors, the Millerites came down from their night on the mountain to reenter a world they'd left long before, a world whose rhythms in time were alien to them. They returned to their communities, where they learned to live without the comfort of a known and certain judgment. Those who kept faith became Seventh-Day Adventists and worked to call others to belief in a slow, gradual apocalypse.

Theirs is a transition that those of us who are interested in the future of the planet would do well to emulate.

Some Brief Speculations on the
Popularity of Entropy as Metaphor

First, a confession: I read Thomas Kuhn's *Structure of Scientific Revolutions* my senior year in college and was so excited by it that I talked about it endlessly. (I'm sure I bear some part of the blame for turning *paradigm* into the archetypal buzzword of the eighties.) I was persuaded well beyond the argument Kuhn actually makes that science rests on nothing more objective than the arbitrary say-so of scientists, who (it seemed to me then) form a narrow-minded, self-selected, self-perpetuating club. If our ecological problems result from pairing science with technology to form the juggernaut of industrial progress, a strong dose of Kuhn, I thought, would break its momentum. His book challenged the very objectivity of science. He could help us see that scientific progress was neither true nor right nor rationally foreordained. *The Structure of Scientific Revolutions* carried the argument against "single vision and Newton's sleep" (as Blake called it) right into the lair of science itself. If everyone would read Kuhn, they would see: we had more choices than we thought.

Throughout graduate school I persevered in this belief and took it even further. My reading of Paul Feyerabend's *Against Method* ("Outline of an Anarchistic Theory of Knowledge," the subtitle announced) soon had me celebrating a relativism in which Ptolemy and Copernicus were equals, in which the fundamental assumptions underlying particle physics had no greater claim to validity than, say, those behind scholastic philosophy or acupuncture or chiropractic or even—the momentum of my principles—New Age crystal therapy. How many angels can dance on the head of a pin? In pre-Kuhnian history of science, the question stands as an example of the absurdity of medieval thought, of its constraint by faith and unexamined assumptions. Angels, pinheads: systematic irrelevance. But how many electrons can dance on the head of a pin? In the modern world this question isn't absurd; it has investigative force. "The thing is," I would say whenever I could get the conversation turned round to Kuhn, "I've never seen an angel *or* an electron. No one has. All anyone sees is evidence of their passage. What you believe determines what you see." Science and scholasticism I made metaphysical equals, just like that.

As between the heliocentric and the geocentric vision of the universe the choice is indeed a toss-up. Each is a perfectly logical system capable of precise mathematical elaboration. They just happen to pivot around a different immovable reference point. But I no longer take celestial mechanics as the paradigm for all of science. My epistemological relativism gradually came to grief on the second law of thermodynamics, which can't be dismissed as an arbitrary or historically determined or subjective construction. Physicist Arthur Eddington spoke with more than a socially and historically contingent validity when he said, "The law that entropy always increases holds, I think, the supreme position among the laws of nature. If someone points out to you that your pet theory of the universe is in disagreement with Maxwell's equations—then so much the worse for Maxwell's equations. If it is found to be contradicted by observation—well, these experimentalists do bungle things sometimes. But if your theory is found to be against the second law of thermodynamics, there is nothing for it but to collapse in deepest humiliation."

The second law, I've come to believe, is one of the bedrock truths about how the universe works. We dismiss it at our peril. It was discovered—invented, if you prefer—by a nineteenth-century

French artillery officer who first articulated it in a guidebook meant to enlighten prospective steam engine owners on the relative merits of different designs. While it certainly smacks of its anthropomorphic origins, it transcends those origins to encapsulate profound, unimpeachable truth.

What is the second law? In one of its more accessible guises, the law of entropy holds that energy spontaneously degrades from more useful to less useful forms, even if it accomplishes no work in the process. It tells us that in any transformation of energy some part of the energy is irretrievably lost to us. The energy doesn't disappear. As the first law of thermodynamics tells us, matter and energy are neither created nor destroyed, only transformed. In an entropic transformation, what is at first "free" energy ("free" in the sense of available, ready to accomplish work) becomes "bound" energy (energy that, like the enormous amount of heat energy contained in the world's oceans, cannot be used to accomplish work).

To give a mundane example: your coffee cools off, infinitesimally raising the temperature of the surrounding air. The heat energy it once contained does not disappear, but has become so dispersed that it is inaccessible and therefore useless. You could gather that energy back together (with, for instance, a heat pump—a refrigerator with an open door, a machine to suck all the heat out of one space and concentrate it in another) only at the cost of a greater expenditure of energy than you could ever hope to recoup. Entropy is the law enforcing an ultimate physical limit—to life, to economy—because it says, in effect, that energy cannot be recycled. Used once, energy is degraded and is never available to us at that level again.

In addition to this fairly accessible aspect of the law of entropy there are others: corollaries that reach to fundamental issues of order and disorder, of probability, of time, of the nature of all change and all transformation. For the law of entropy is also a law of probability, holding that in any spontaneous transformation improbable order succumbs to more probable chaos. It further suggests that this is how we know earlier from later states; entropy is why we know time. The law of entropy is unique among physical laws for describing an irreversible process, and because of that the science of thermodynamics as it evolved in the mid-nineteenth century challenged the clarity and comprehensiveness of Newtonian mechanism. (Blake's path beyond Newton began with a step toward mysticism. Einstein's path beyond Newton began with a step into thermodynamics.)

To see how this is so, imagine a movie of a purely mechanical process—say, of the inner workings of a gearbox. The movie offers no clues as to whether it is being run forward or backward. Only if the frame enlarges to include the source of energy that drives the gears can we tell in which direction the movie is being projected, for no engine can convert motion and heat into gasoline. (If an engine could do that, we'd have no need to drill for oil, no oil depletion allowance, no inflation driven by the increasing energy cost of energy, no energy problems whatsoever.) And more generally, antientropic occurrences so confound our normal experience that their representation in this way—water falling uphill, broken eggs pulling themselves together and jumping up into a waiting hand—is a source of fascination and delight. Because our subjective experience of time is intimately connected with the second law, it's fair to call it, with Eddington (and Martin Amis), "time's arrow."

Entropy was the first general physical law to be explicitly probabilistic in character, and this too was a challenge to the mechanical certainty of Newtonian, classical physics. The French philosopher Henri Bergson called the law of entropy "the most metaphysical law of nature." It *is* undeniably difficult to grasp. Nicholas Georgescu-Roegen, a Romanian-born economist who makes use of the law as a foundation for his radical reinterpretation of economic experience, notes that even physicists have difficulty comprehending it.

Opacity is an invitation to projection. Almost from the moment of its inception the second law has enjoyed widespread popularity as metaphor, exercising a compelling attraction well beyond the confines of physics, and it was this currency that first drew my attention to it in graduate school. The second law turns up in the

oddest places, creating—like metaphor itself—provocatively jux-
taposed bedfellows. There it is, evident in a sheaf of poets: Swin-
burne ("Then star nor sun shall waken / Nor any change of light")
and Frost ("I am a sleepless / Slowfaring eater / Maker of rust and
rot"), Yeats ("The center cannot hold"), and Eliot ("This is the way
the world ends / This is the way the world ends / This is the way the
world ends / Not with a bang but a whimper"). Not just poets but
political theorists, cranks and economists, novelists and historians,
philosophers and pop psychologists—all manner of thinkers have
latched on to entropy as useful metaphor. What sort of idea is it
that is turned to account by such a disparate group?

I began collecting references to the second law, and eventually
my idle curiosity became an academically enforced obsession as I
made the social history of the second law the topic of my doctoral
dissertation. I found that some of the law's employers had been
drawn not just to entropy's complexity and to the support it appears
to lend to a stylish, dark-browed pessimism, but also (ironically
enough) to what Coleridge might have called the idea's esemplas-
tic or unifying power. That is, many of entropy's metaphoric uses
go beyond "mere" metaphor to become what philosopher Stephen
Pepper (Thomas Kuhn's mentor) called basic or root metaphor: a
central image, understood as literal truth, which serves as the foundation image of a worldview, a paradigm, or (in Pepper's terms)
a world theory of unlimited scope—a theory, more or less consciously held, that tries to encompass everything.

It's a concept easiest to understand through example. Pepper
found four world theories alive and well in the western tradition,
each grounded in a different root metaphor, each forming a distinct
school or subtradition of thought. Mechanism takes the mechanical system as its archetypal real thing and sees in the objects of our
experience collections of removable, manipulable parts that are
related by clear, rigid principles of cause and effect. To partisans
of this metaphor (Democritus, Descartes, Hobbes, Locke, Berkeley,
and Hume), anything that can't be modeled as a mechanical system
is not real.

Organicism takes the living organism as its exemplar. It contradicts the atomism of mechanism by asserting that the whole is greater than the sum of its parts and is therefore the more appropriate unit of analysis. The paradigmatic organicist is Hegel. James Lovelock, whose Gaia hypothesis suggests that the world's ecology is best seen as one enormous, self-regulating living organism, is firmly in this tradition.

Formism conceives of reality in mathematician's terms. What is true and real and essential for it are formulae (or more generally the formal relations that formulae transcribe), not the particular things that come into being and pass away and are, during their existence, measured with those formulae. Formism takes the abstract concept of similarity as its basic image. It holds that the bedrock of reality isn't matter (material things are too temporary and changeable to be real) but form itself. Typical partisans are Plato, Aristotle, and those scholastic philosophers endlessly debating and distinguishing formal categories; in the modern era you might include among Formists those theoretic physicists searching for a Grand Unified Theory, the ultimate, transcendentally true mathematical form.

Finally, Contextualism takes the artistic enterprise as its paradigmatic model and elaborates a central imagery of relations (between purpose and media, foreground and background, artist and environment) and creative process. Pepper finds it in the works of pragmatists and vitalists such as Peirce, James, Bergson, Dewey, and Mead.

The root metaphor of "entropism" is not a variant of any of these. Indeed, it bears a striking similarity to a kind of root metaphor that Pepper dismissed as inadequate, the root metaphor of generating substance. World theories built on this root metaphor are most obvious in the works of the pre-Socratics, many of whom believed that the apparent diversity of substance in the world is illusory, since all that exists must have been generated from one primordial substance. Thales, for instance, believed that "all is water"—a statement the modern mind tends to interpret as metaphor in order to save a founder of philosophy from an obvious absurdity. But Thales spoke literally. Long before modern particle physics and its search for the essential building blocks of matter, he apparently argued himself by logical steps to the idea that behind the many there is, there must be, a One. His pupil Anaximander thought that water was rather crude as an essential substance and substituted for it the apeiron, an infinite mixture of all things, and added the explanatory concept of "shaking out" to explain how particular qualities were congealed into the various objects of the world. Pythagoras, combining the generating substance metaphor with formism, thought all was number.

Pepper says that to partisans of this kind of world theory all things fall into one of three categories: "(1) a generating substance (or maybe several), (2) principles of change like 'shaking out' and rarefaction-condensation, and (3) generated substances produced by (1) through (2)." The problem, Pepper thought, was that this root metaphor has inadequate scope. It can't account very well for the diversity of phenomena in the world, but must dismiss a great deal of what is as illusion, as being essentially unreal.

As a modern incarnation of this world theory Entropism finds energy (or one of its cognate terms: low entropy, order, negentropy, information) to be the generating substance and the law of entropy to be the primary principle of change. The daily working lives of astrophysicists and nuclear engineers, who regularly see demonstrated the transubstantiation of energy into matter and matter into energy, suggest that Pepper was premature in dismissing the generating substance metaphor as unsatisfactory.

As the root metaphor of a world theory of unlimited scope, the idea of entropy serves the same function within the work of some nineteenth- and twentieth-century thinkers that Newtonian mechanism served in the eighteenth and early nineteenth centuries: it stands as an unchallengeable truth with a content applicable to all phenomena, all relation, all matters of fact. Just as Plato applied the categories and terms of the highest science of his time, Pythagoreanism, to the polity, and just as Hobbes thought to outline a Newtonian politics suited to a clockwork cosmos and a clockwork psychology ("What is the *heart* but a *spring;* and the nerves, but so many *strings?*"), so did some nineteenth- and twentieth-century thinkers try to compress the social and political world under the categories of thermodynamics. Thus, for instance, the idea of entropy served as the foundation of Brooks Adams's economic theory of history in *The Law of Civilization and Decay,* and as an organizing metaphor in his brother Henry's more literary philosophy of history. Brooks Adams used the metaphor with diligent literalness, hoping to find in such categories as racial and cultural energy the roots of a scientific approach to history. Henry distanced himself from the metaphor, seeing it somewhat paradoxically as both the product and prophet of science as an agent of social decline.

A decade later, in the 1900s, Wilhelm Ostwald found a moral content lurking in the second law and used it to justify his categorical imperative: "Waste no energy!" As a guiding principle, that imperative led Ostwald to work for the adoption of Esperanto as an international language (translation was a needless waste of energy) and to advocate the industrial and economic efficiencies that could be achieved through an internationally federated technocracy run by a scientific elite. That elite, maintained through a worldwide eugenics program (reproduction by inferior specimens was also a needless waste of energy), was to manage our scarce calories for the greatest good of the greatest number—a vision that was, to Ostwald, the logical development of a revelatory, essentially religious moment of insight in which he perceived that "all is energy."

More recently, thermodynamics led some popular writers to a social vision diametrically opposed to Ostwald's. In the late 1970s Jeremy Rifkin and Hazel Henderson both found in the idea of entropy the ultimate justification for a New Age politics of grassroots decentralization and a New Age economics that values the handmade, homegrown, and durable over the store-bought, plastic, and disposable. Both lean on Nicholas Georgescu-Roegen's work in macroeconomic theory in advancing their cases, but there is an important difference between his work and theirs. Georgescu-Roegen, in arguing that our mania for perpetual economic growth must someday come up hard against the truths of thermodynamics, confines himself to a literal use of the entropy law, while Rifkin and Henderson are led into the realm of metaphor when they use the law of entropy to model what they describe as our current social and political malaise. Neither admits the metaphor. Like Thales and his water, Plato and form, or Hobbes and the great machine, Rifkin and Henderson clearly believe themselves to be speaking literal truth.

Rifkin and Henderson can be seen as constituting a contemporary reprise of Brooks Adams. All three were led by the organizing power of the idea of entropy to speak of cultural and political energy (and its dissipation in entropic processes) in their efforts to establish a continuity of explanation between culture and its material basis in nature.

Henry Adams, too, has his contemporary parallel in the person of Thomas Pynchon who explicitly modeled a character after the elder Adams in his short story "Entropy," first published in 1960. Pynchon's second and third novels—*The Crying of Lot 49* in 1966 and *Gravity's Rainbow* in 1973—inhabit the metaphoric ground of the second law in offering their readers a new mythos by which to understand modern industrial culture. There are differences between the novels: *Lot 49* is brief, and (as one pair of critics pointed out) it offers readers a participatory myth of a redemptive subculture; by the time we finish reading it, "we are all members of Tristero," the centuries-old private postal system that figures in the story, an invisible, anarchic network, a kind of preelectronic Internet, by which many Americans "truly communicate, whilst reserving their lies, their recitations of routine, their arid betrayals of spiritual poverty" for the official postal system.

In contrast, *Gravity's Rainbow* is a massive, dark, encyclopedic novel, which (like *Lot 49*) dances along the sometimes broad, sometimes fine line that separates paranoia from political theory, but which offers us no easy path to redemption. Characters are embedded in their private manias, and paranoid "we systems" constitute the main form of human connection. Common to both novels, though, is a use of the idea of entropy as metaphor that is similar to the elder Adams's. Unlike Rifkin, Henderson, and Brooks Adams, both Pynchon and Henry Adams are consciously turning a metaphor in their use of the idea of entropy as an organizing image.

Such uses—which range from C. P. Snow's appeal to the second law as the test of the existence of "Two Cultures," to the Soviet physicist M. A. Markov's likening of an arms race to the process by which an iron poker, heated until red-hot at one end, becomes painfully hot at the other—show that the second law has become embedded in our culture's collective imagination to a remarkable degree. I think that this popularity can be plumbed for meaning. What are the reasons for it? What do those reasons say about our culture and its understanding of itself?

First, entropy connotes disorder. If, as Sheldon Wolin says in *Politics and Vision,* during times of political disorder the accepted modes of thought are called into question, we might also suspect that those who wish to question accepted modes of thought perceive the world to be on the brink of chaos. The use of the idea of entropy as a metaphor for society or history could thus be a sign that the root metaphor by which we understand ourselves is changing—or that those who employ it want to see our root metaphor changed. (Our root metaphor need not change to entropism. The second law may be a transitional metaphor, mediating change to another.)

Second, entropy is obviously pessimistic. Its use as a metaphor is a convenient shorthand for articulating a sense that things are running downhill, falling apart, getting worse. Its popularity is thus related to the cult of nostalgia that modern culture calls forth as a reaction and then exploits: in the commercial experiences offered as escape (Disney World opens into a sanitized version of "Main Street, U.S.A." circa 1880), in advertising (on television curmudgeonly old grocers, bakers, vintners, and pharmacists hawk the wares of modern conglomerates from quaint country stores), in politics (Reagan set the example here, achieving great popularity by aiming squarely at the past, evoking a simpler era of wholesome living and apparently clear-cut distinctions: communist or free, able-bodied or lazy, American or inferior).

Entropy is also popular because, third, it is a vague idea, difficult to understand, in part because it is difficult to picture. In a classic statement of the mechanist's creed Lord Kelvin once asserted that the mind can't comprehend what it can't picture or model in mechanical terms. As a fundamentally antimechanist principle, entropy would on this reading be incomprehensible. As it is, the vagueness of the idea means that its "system of associated commonplaces" (philosopher Max Black) has a large penumbra. That vagueness is an invitation to metaphoric use. It also suits political reality. Despite the reductive, simplifying tendencies of televisualized campaigning (in which the typical candidate, bidding to become a lawgiver for the ages, stays "on message" in fifteen-second chunks), in actual policymaking practice the clarity of simple distinction dissipates in the face of complex experience. We can no longer hear an oxymoron in the term *domestic terrorist*. Ecologists call for hunting seasons on moose, deer, and geese; duck hunters are incontrovertibly the planet's best champions of ducks and duck habitat. Women gain individual control of their reproductive lives at the exact historical moment that overpopulation leads us back toward the idea that, because mammalian population growth is a function of female fertility, society has some degree of interest in what happens in every human womb. More and more of our policy problems reveal themselves to be true dilemmas—not the product of a historic struggle between good *here* and evil *there* but the result of a complex competition between desirable, incompatible goods. Entropy seems appropriately to model the murk.

Fourth: we live in an energy-conscious age. An energy-conscious age makes of the notion of energy a popular metaphor, and where there is energy, there is entropy. It's the process that insulation attempts to slow down. Nearly every handbook on solar design or energy-efficient retrofit contains a brief exposition of the idea. In a 1970s contribution to the literature on popular science, Harold J.

Morowitz identified five general uses of the term *energy:* (1) the simple thermodynamic definition ("ability to do work or to cause motion"); (2) a sort of bodily vigor ("if only I had the energy, I could plant a garden like that"); (3) a derivative of the oriental notion of bodily tone, as in the theory behind acupuncture; (4) the psychic energy of the libido, manifest in drives; and (5) spiritual strength or vitality. Only the first of these can be denominated in calories; entropy edges over into metaphor when applied to any of the others.

A fifth reason for the popularity of the entropy metaphor is that it can seem to lend the authority of science to an argument or image. There are several reasons for this being a source of appeal. Despite Kuhn—or, more exactly, despite a host of relativizing postmodernists who make use of his work in their efforts to "delegitimize science as one of the primary metanarratives supporting sexual and racial oppression"—science is and remains the main stock of apparently certain knowledge in our culture. Thermodynamics has displaced Newtonian mechanics as its fundament. If, as Michael Walzer suggested in the June 1967 issue of *Political Science Quarterly,* thinkers are "driven to escape" from disciplines in which knowledge is less certain in order to find a point of fixity in an authoritative realm, which can then be imported, through metaphor, into the original field, we shouldn't be surprised to find political and social thinkers turning to thermodynamics as a source of analogy, image, and metaphor.

But the entropy metaphor appeals even to those who view science as a source of much evil in the world. That appeal need not always be ironic, as it was for Henry Adams, or a sign of a lack of thought, as it seems to be for some of the entropy metaphor's more recent popularizers. Behind the appeal of the entropy metaphor is an attenuated form of the fallacy of clearing the ground. If science itself can be made, through the entropy metaphor, to suggest that a culture based on science is in decline, the way seems clear for alternatives. Technically, according to the strictest interpretation of forensic principles, the demonstration of the shortcomings of one theory has no bearing on the attempt to demonstrate the value or worth of another. But here logical technique falls short. With world visions we are not so much concerned to demonstrate their truth or falsity in some absolute sense as we are concerned to argue for their appropriateness. Since this is a matter of relative degree, clearing the ground can be an acceptable rhetorical strategy. Entropy thus has, for some modern Luddites, all the appeal of the *tue quoque* ("What about you?") form of argument.

I think in this we glimpse a relic of an essential human nature, a kind of ideational totemism. If you gain the strength of a lion by eating of its muscle, so that you can hunt it, perhaps you gain an advantage on science by partaking of its ideas and using them as metaphor.

A sixth reason: the entropy process itself is omnipresent. It lies behind all change in the physical world. Death, decay, rust, rot— these are obvious manifestations. Less obviously, but no less justifiably, one may detect the specter of the second law behind such mundane activities as housework, eating, routine maintenance chores, splitting wood (or—less mundanely—atoms), purchasing fuel, or changing a light bulb. Even the sublime is not free from entropic connotations. In the germination of a seed we can be reminded that all life supports itself by sorting low entropy (valuable matter and energy) from its environment. (Indeed, this is an effective definition of a live thing, this capacity to sort low entropy, to leave a high-entropy wake through time.) Much of our purposive activity individually and collectively is directed toward resisting the entropic decline of those things we value. We can't overcome it— within any closed system, entropy must ever increase—but we can cause the net entropy gain to take place "out there," in nature, that vast storage dump. "Entropy is a law of dynamics," not merely thermodynamics, Georgescu-Roegen tells us. Wherever there is change, there is entropy.

A seventh reason is suggested by James Hillman's work, especially his notion that metaphor is a "minimyth" and myth is a "comprehensive metaphor." The incidence of metaphor in our thought and speech—especially the regular, systemic uses of a pattern of relational imagery that characterize root metaphor—may be a sign that we haven't left and may never completely leave behind mythic forms in our effort to understand ourselves and our world. Entropy as metaphor is a peculiar mix: a sort of compromise between scientific rationality and (given that the full implications of the idea are rarely understood by those who use it as metaphor) inscrutable magic.

Entropy is a law of nature, and to see it at work in the affairs of humans is to suggest (eighth) that those affairs are beyond our control. What we can't control we can't have responsibility for; just as technology is an "ethical armor," distancing us from the impact of our activities so that the causal connections (and hence responsibility for consequences) are obscured, entropy as metaphoric mirror reflects our sense of helplessness. "When a supervisor victimizes a worker, a terrible entropy often results in a wife being beaten," writes Hugh Drummond, a psychologist interested in clarifying modern human relations. Thus do we learn, through entropy as metaphor, to speak in a passive voice.

Humans have always worshipped a god of Order and feared the dark agency of Chaos, and this is another source of entropy's appeal. While an important minority voice in history has celebrated the liberating quality of chaos (Bakunin, for example), that celebration values chaos only as a precondition for discerning new forms of order. Dramatic social change has always been mediated by an appeal to a different (sometimes more subtle, sometimes an as-yet-unknowable) form of order. God and Satan; the elect and the damned or the self-righteous and the humble preterit; the free market and special interests or rational planning and private greed; good patriots and fifth columnists or jingoistic nationalists and a critical, thoughtful citizenry—these are the pairs of dialectical pairs through which we cast our vision of the ideal order and through which we generate our explanations of the failure of reality to achieve the ideal. To the malevolent powers in the world we may now add entropy, the modern force for disorder. Its complement is energy, the organizing principle that maintains the integrity of the structures and systems through which it flows.

Entropy as malevolent power suggests a tenth reason for its popularity as metaphor. We crave narratives with simple villains, epic struggle, and flattering self-portraits, and entropy can seem to oblige. In *The Road Less Traveled,* M. Scott Peck explains it all for us. Entropy, he says, means the universe is running down. But intelligent life exists. How could this be? Something must be thrusting up against this force of entropy, struggling against it, defying natural law, struggling up from the simplest virus, through bacteria and the one-cells, into fish and birds and animals and, finally, into Man, "the most complex but least numerous organism." And what is that grand, struggling something, the thing that confounds the second law? "Natural law as yet undefined," he tells us, nothing other than the spirituality inherent in our race. Mmmmm. More properly, a thermodynamically enlightened ecology teaches that the increasing complexity and differentiation seen in evolution are in no sense antientropic but are its logical result. Entropy dictates competition for scarce food calories, a competition that drives evolution. As a principle of disorder, entropy accounts for the random variations introduced in the transmission of genetic information from parents to offspring. Random variation, accrued over epochs: evolution is not directed toward producing us. It is not directed toward any end at all. The slightest brush with ecology or physics would have taught Peck that no process in nature or culture can contradict the law of entropy. The entropy account is always balanced somewhere. If such tutoring were inconvenient, he could have gone for a walk or perhaps picked up a newspaper. Either could have shown him that humans, complex though they are, are by no means a uniquely complex animal or the least numerous organism we have here on earth. The epic tale here is not of spirit vanquishing entropy but of Peck's ignorance. He's taught millions of readers pure pseudo-thermodynamic drivel.

Law of chaos is an oxymoron, and in the tension that it (and probability theory in general) encompasses we have another clue to the popularity of entropy as metaphor. While we know that the forces of darkness can never be eradicated, and never fully predicted, we have made them scrutable. The law of entropy thus functions as a talisman.

This dialectical tension suggests yet a twelfth source of the metaphor's appeal: the success of humanity's domination of nature. We once knew nature as chaos, a threatening realm of indefinite danger, and we walled our cities against it. Now the roles are reversed. Culture threatens nature, and the wilderness that is left is found in tiny pockets surrounded by fence and farm. "Nature"—a Janus-faced ideal, embodying both the orderly and the chaotic—has itself become an endangered species. As immanence in the world, it has been brought to the brink of extinction by the plow and the pressure of human population. As pure concept, as an element in the human imagination, it has been tamed by science (which illuminates its prolific relations and reveals their regularity, forcing them to yield up their logic to our inquiry) and history (which shows us that over and over what we humans have perceived as natural is, instead, the product of our ideas at a particular moment in time).

Sometimes it seems that all the chaos that is left to us is the chaos of our own devising. As Wolfgang Giegerich has pointed out, our nuclear weaponry constitutes a potential for instantaneous disorder as unprecedented in history as the thoroughness of our domination of nature. (Is there then a first law of chaos, a law of the conservation of disorder?) In taming nature we have traded the high magic that can be found in the transcendent union of the logos and the void for the low paradox of "wilderness management," and gained no net security in the bargain. If humans have a need to experience a dialectical tension between order and disorder—between the knowable and the recondite, the predictable and the risky, the transparent and the mysterious—is it any wonder that the law of entropy appeals to the imagination of a culture that finds it necessary to manage wilderness bureaucratically—and to issue permits to those who sojourn there? In the idea of chaos, it seems, lies our last best hope of possibility: of breaking loose the cultural bonds and definitions that constrain our relations to self, to others, to the world, as we must on occasion if we are to remain sane and authentic. Entropy as root metaphor recaptures something of the psychic economy of the walled city, for it tells us that the elements of culture are statistically improbable and temporally parochial pockets of order in a world that marches toward maximum chaos. It is, on the whole, better than the concrete chaos of Armageddon. But as a shadow reality, abstract, invisible, and not quite immanent in our world, it is poor consolation.

Can thermodynamics provide a nonrelativist, post-Kuhn grounding for a new, ecologically enlightened world? Perhaps. Clearly an appreciation of the physics of energy is one large step toward understanding "nature's economy," the web of ecological relation that strains to include humans and their economy. But all really rich metaphors allow for contradictory applications, as Susan Sontag (*Illness as Metaphor*) has pointed out. Entropy suggests both that the human struggle for order is hopeless and that we can achieve order by living in harmony with the forms of order that the sun's energy helped to create and supports. The one becomes a justification either for abandoning the conquest of nature or for pursuing it with greater energy. The second might, with a bit of luck, lead us toward a saner, more ecological society.

On Hunting

stranger walks the shoulder of State Route 14, a two-lane road that winds north through the hills of Vermont from Barre ("Granite Capital of the World") toward Hardwick ("Gateway to the Northeast Kingdom"). He wears a red and black plaid wool jacket, a bright orange peakless cap, and green wool trousers. He is portly. Firmly bound to one shoulder is the leather strap of a rifle, and its barrel protrudes upward, a long thin snorkel bobbing above his head. It gives him a vaguely amphibious air. As I pass him at something near the regulation fifty miles an hour I can see that this hike is straining him. His cheeks are red and he seems, in the short glance I have of him, to be out of breath.

There is something anomalous about a man walking along a road with a rifle. To those with urban reflexes the sight is likely to quicken the heart and sharpen the senses, for in a world of pavement and glass a man with a gun can mean only danger. Even when there is no danger—even in open country where this sight is not unusual, even when the rifle is strapped to a wool-clad shoulder and pointed innocuously at the sky—there is something disconcerting about the vision. The man is a hunter. His presence here along the road means he isn't hunting. He is out of place, away from the activity that defines him.

Hunting is an uncivil activity. It occurs outside the boundaries of civic organization, in a landscape whose distance from the city can't be measured solely by the space that lies between the hunter and the nearest high-rise apartment. The city depends on agriculture. As Marx taught us, the farmer's fields are a necessary antipode to the apartment building; the character of one determines the character of the other. There would be no tranquil, pastoral Vermont without there being, somewhere over the horizon, The City: New York, Boston, Montreal, economic engines whose torrential streams of income ripple and eddy up here as surely as dry autumn leaves fly in the wake of my car.

In its essence hunting is a stranger to both farm and city, a stranger to the form of order that is represented in the plow and structural steel. While our agricultural society has domesticated the hunt, turning it variously into a formal and mannered social occasion or a democratic, somewhat plebeian escape from routine, true hunters—those whose lives depend on success in the hunt—survive today only in lands that no farming tribe has ever contested, lands in which the urban dominion that wraps the globe takes the form of a thin and tenuous jurisdiction over wilderness. For most of recorded history there has been animosity between farming peoples and hunting peoples. The farmers have tended to see the animosity as being rooted in the pure uncivilized savagery of the hunter. To the hunter, the problem was always a basic incompatibility of religious vision, manifest in the farmer's penchant for ownership and control, which to the hunter are forms of desecration.

An appreciation of the hunter's point of view in this, the conflict that led to the first and longest of all world wars, is a relatively recent development in western culture. You don't need to have read Marx to see that the appreciation is neither accidental nor entirely innocent of self-interest. As agriculture has expanded its dominion, making use of the industrial powers it helped to liberate, its shortcomings, written larger, have become more apparent—a state of affairs that seduces us into romanticizing the simplicity and nobility of the hunter and gatherer.

But romantic idealization is meager reparation for four thousand years of genocide. (Desire rarely does justice to its object.) Because romanticism depends upon the form of memory (and the sense of loss) that comes from seeing time as an infinite series of unique moments that can never recur, it does not escape history—it depends upon our linear march toward mortality to lend life its poignant, shadow-tinged sweetness.

This linear idea of history is one part of what's at issue in the conflict between hunters and gatherers and agriculturalists. History was not only written by the winners, it was *invented* by them, and its imposition on the world was a crucial component of the injustice that agriculturalists visited on hunting tribes, most of whom inhabited a universe in which no action was ever completely novel. For preliterate hunting tribes, all of life had precedent, and every action had its place within a cyclical and repetitive vision of time. Hunters and gatherers walked (always) metaphorically and (often) literally in the footsteps of their ancestors. Today our romantic idealization of the paleo-hunter only serves to affirm the completeness of the farmer's victory. The secure victor can afford to be indulgent, even generous. Victory brings to the customs, beliefs, and mores of the vanquished a certain charm and interest.

And yet there is a paradox here, one that Hegel, Marx's antecedent as a dialectical thinker, might have appreciated. Geologic time with its apparently infinite stretches represents the fullest extrapolation of the historical consciousness invented by the farmer. But geologic time transcends the mind-set that marks off days and hours and minutes. It boggles the mental constructs of human time as it is lived. In so doing it offers a near replication of the hunter's immersion in cyclic and sacred time; each is a transcendence of mundane linearity. And, to one mindful of geologic time, agriculture and the urban life it supports can be recognized as recent experiments in social organization, experiments that may yet demonstrate the wisdom of peoples we once viewed as savage.

No one would mistake my portly hunter for a savage. Like most of the deer hunters in Vermont he is only a commuter to the terri-

tory of the hunt. But at least he has been in the woods and has seen
what can be seen there. Whenever an alien culture intrudes on ours
there's incongruity, even when the intrusion is as mild as this, a
part-time hunter walking the graveled shoulder of a stretch of two-
lane blacktop, far from the centers of the urban culture that produced the road, closer to the woods in which the city's bonds seem
loosened.

Hunters are men, mostly. (According to a census by the U.S. Fish
and Wildlife Service, of the 17.5 million Americans who hunted in
1980, only 8 percent were women. That number has been rising,
but men are as yet in no danger of being put in the minority.) And
while they pursue a variety of game, it is the pursuit of the white-
tail deer, *Odocoileus virginianus,* that most often defines them in
the public mind. The white-tail's range is continental, and it's the
largest animal taken in any great number in this country. They're
ranked as big game, almost in spite of the fact that they are so plen-
tiful. If the culture is drawn to the symbolism of the large, hunters
are, too. For many, hunting means deer hunting, and deer season is
the event toward which the year moves.

Hunting is not a spectator sport. There aren't any vicarious thrills
in hunting, unless they're found in the emotions the hunter feels
when his quarry escapes or is killed. No one pays money to watch
another person hunt. The few attempts at presenting hunting on
television have been dismal failures, scarcely drawing audiences,
even on slow and rainy Sundays. This is not just because the presence of a camera and crew distorts the activity, so that the hunting
that can be shown on television is not the hunting that actually is.
Hunting is a peculiarly private, if not always strictly solitary, act.
We see hunters only when they have ceased hunting, only when
they emerge from the woods. In the towns of Vermont during deer
season they congregate in the parking lots of general stores, eating
their lunches while the rest of the social world does its morning
commute to work. They stand outside, drinking coffee or liquor
against the chill of sitting motionless in the autumn woods. They

gather to talk, to compare, to commiserate, to mock, and above all to tell stories.

In the group that stands one morning outside the Plainfield General Store there's a man whose hands gesture easily, moving fluidly on forearms that are pinioned against the hood of his pickup truck, which the group is using as a coffee table. Now and again he thumps the dusty hood of the truck for emphasis, shaking the styrofoam cups, threatening the roast beef sandwich that lies close at hand atop its plastic wrap. They are a raucous and burly lot, and were it not for the fact that my friend Frank has introduced me to a few of them I just might feel a little ill at ease as I pass on my way into the store.

Mine is a discomfort that others share. Every autumn, during deer season, many of my friends and acquaintances become indignant. For some the indignity has to do with loss of services. A large proportion of the native population here hunts, so much so that if it weren't for the urban refugees (the majority of whom are members of the professions), the economy would come to a grinding halt. As it is commerce suffers, and everyone comes to understand that certain things are impossible during deer season: you can't get your car repaired today, you can't get that extra insurance cord of wood delivered before it snows, you can't get a plumber or an electrician or a fuel-oil delivery this week. But others have a resentment whose origin lies deeper than mere inconvenience. For two weeks the hunters have the run of the woods. There are complicated rules for posting your land against hunters, and any shortcoming in your execution of the directions gives license for their access. For two weeks, hunters are an unavoidable presence in much of the public space of rural Vermont, not only at general stores but also on the backroads, where they are found walking or waiting and where their vehicles appear before dawn, parked in high weeds or tucked into small clearings and old logging roads, abandoned for the day, a temporary litter of metal marking the passage of predators like so much mechanical scat.

If you feel a sense of ownership of the woods it isn't hard to see hunters as an invading force. Many people resent the feeling of insecurity their presence creates, and some would like to prevent these men with guns from killing "defenseless" animals. But in this belief they transpose their knowledge of domesticated animals onto the wild. Deer haven't been selectively bred for stupidity, and they aren't at all defenseless. As wild herbivores their primary defenses are stealth and flight, strategies so successful that fewer than 10 percent of the hunters here take home any meat.

In their attitudes toward hunting, antihunters reflect the conventions of our culture and their class. Most of them have grown up with a Walt Disney version of nature. In the moral universe of our culture's folk tales and children's stories, herbivores are always innocent, carnivores always dangerous or downright evil. It could hardly be otherwise for an agricultural tribe. Most antihunters come from (or aspire to mimic) the great urban middle class, and part of their disquiet comes from the sheer uncivilized earthiness of hunting. They bring with them an image of nature as a tranquil, pastoral scene—much like a city park, or the close-cropped pastures of a Vermont dairy farm—and they've been taught that it isn't quite polite to dwell on bodily functions. Hunting reminds them a bit too directly that humans are animals, that some animals eat other animals, that gore, blood, excrement, and death are natural, as natural as clouds, pasture, amber waves of grain.

Once, at a dinner party, the vice president of a local college told me that it is immoral for a person to hunt if that person can afford to buy meat. This is a popular belief. The middle class, it seems, would forgive the poverty stricken—for whom a hundred pounds of venison can represent a sizable addition to a food budget—but would enforce their morals on their own. No doubt the vice president thought he was being understanding of the role that hunting plays in the traditional economy of a rural area by adapting his moral absolute to financial circumstance.

I can afford meat. I hunt.

I tried to explain myself to him.

There is, of course, an obvious hypocrisy involved in the belief that killing is immoral if you can afford to pay someone to do it for you. More difficult to answer are the committed vegetarians, who avoid meat for health or moral reasons. Sometimes we find common ground. I, too, am wary of chemical additives. I, too, dislike the indignities that are perpetrated on animals by factory farming. It seems to me more noble, I suggest to them, to pursue and eventually eat an animal that has not been denied its freedom, has not been genetically manipulated or chemically bloated, but is instead wholly other, occupying an ecological niche that its ancestors, and not we humans, have defined. I try to explain how it is that I believe the world would be a better place if more people hunted—if more of our food calories came from hunting and gathering.

Anthropology supports me: hunting and gathering tribes are less bloodthirsty toward their own species than agricultural tribes. Thermodynamics supports me: industrial agriculture is extremely wasteful of energy, using on the average twenty calories for every calorie of food delivered to the consumer. Natural and organic farming techniques are better—some of these at least have a positive caloric income—but the most efficient food delivery systems that humans have ever known have been those of hunters and gatherers. I talk about the mind-set of control that begins with agriculture—control that begins with the plow (clearly an act of violence against the complex living thing that is a soil community), continues through property relations and ownership of land (an act of violence against the integrity of ecosystems), through the genetic manipulation of domesticated creatures so that they might better suit our ends, and culminates in the most depraved treatment of humans by humans that we can imagine. Only an agricultural tribe, I have been heard to say, could invent concentration camps and practice genocide. Hunters and gatherers have no notion of weeds or "varmints," no tendency to define other creatures as pests, no animus that leads them to see total annihilation of another species or race or way of life as a solution. That amber wave of grain to which the farmer aspires isn't natural but is achieved only through a rigorous program of granting life to one species and energetically denying it to all others—a program that usually includes indiscriminate poisoning and herbal genocide, practices whose moral foundations are a good deal shakier than those of hunting.

Sometimes this argument makes an impression. But still there is the problem of death. Many moral vegetarians have chosen their stance precisely because they want to avoid causing death. Hunting too obviously contradicts the fundament upon which their very selves depend.

I confess to getting impatient with this kind of moral vegetarianism. I think that it, like anorexia, is self-denial in the service of an acculturated pathology. Its main root seems to be an all-too-human hubris that leads the vegetarian to think that antiseptic innocence is possible in this world. In turning away from the ecological niche that shaped our ancestors even as they claimed it, by renouncing the eons of evolution as carnivores that have made us what we are—conscious, self-conscious, erect hominids with binocular vision, opposable thumbs, an ability to symbolize and communicate our experience through language, and a deep-seated faith that the events of our lives have a coherence that can be plumbed for meaning—the moral vegetarian is trying to elect him- or herself out of context. In this, the vegetarian exemplifies the source of our ecological problems no less than the technocrat or engineer, whose disregard for context is founded not on an optimistic faith in the possibility of purity but on an optimistic faith in troubleshooting, a faith that those principles of nature that work to our inconvenience can be made irrelevant through the exercise of more control and more power. The engineer must admit the possibility of failure, of error, of guilt, and so is led away from an excessively romantic self-image. But the proselytizing moral vegetarian, believing in the strength of his or her own example, believes in the possibility of a general and mutual innocence. This is sentimental schmaltz—the kind of sentimentality that is necessary to produce the excessive brutality for which agricultural tribes are known.

No: we humans are inescapably *of* nature. Tragedy and sin have origins in our existence deeper than mere ignorance, and it's arrogance to believe otherwise.

"Let me show you what I got in the mail today." I follow Frank into the living room of the old farm house he rents. "This is Blacktop. I got him last bow season." Kneeling, he strokes a cured deerskin that is flat on the floor. "I call him Blacktop because of this brownish-black tinge here," he adds, indicating the hair roots down the center of the hide, the fur that would have covered the spine. "Want to see pictures of him?" He shows me several photographs. In them, Frank is dressed in his camouflage clothes, though he has removed the camouflage paint from his face for the picture. (The camouflage is necessary to penetrate the deer's fright-and-flight range, and it is the main reason bow hunters have their own hunting season. They don't share the woods with riflemen, who sometimes mistake even uncamouflaged humans for game.) The carcass of the deer is on the ground at his knee. In one hand he holds the bow he used to kill the animal. In the other, he holds one of the animal's antlers, showing the rack to good advantage for the photographer.

Frank shows me the hunting journal he keeps. "August 29. Light frost this morning (55 days since the last frost of spring). From the porch I saw three deer grazing at the edge of the hayfield. One a spikehorn, another with a perfect eight point rack, the last with a fringe of black fur on top. Blacktop is 140 pounds, Perfect Eight 120, Spikehorn less than a 100. They grazed through for twenty minutes, disappeared into Nolfi's woods."

Frank watched for Blacktop throughout the fall, spotting him once a week or so until the season started in November. He recounts the confrontation he witnessed between Perfect Eight and Blacktop just before the rut, when the bucks become territorial. "And then," he says, acting out the role of his deer, "Blacktop says, 'Enough of this,' and rears on his hind legs, still with Perfect Eight locked in his rack, and he shoves him back, just bulldozes him out of the way." For a moment I'm afraid Frank will bulldoze me out of his living room, but he stops short before me. "That's the last I saw of Perfect Eight."

The flesh side of the deerskin has slashes and scuffs at the neck. Did Frank have trouble skinning him? "No," he says. "Feel this— feel the difference between the neck and the skin down here." The skin at the neck is thicker, stiffer. "That's all scar tissue, from years of fighting. The scars go right through. You know how I got him?" Frank is ready to tell me the story. "It was sheer accident. Had nothing to do with skill. It was just luck. Three of us went in the woods, walking into our bow stands, and we came to mine first. I had this stuff on, this imitation fox urine scent, and I was waiting there, waiting in my stand."

I know that every year Frank hangs his hunting clothes outdoors in the rain and weather for the week before hunting season, and then rubs them with cut apples. He bathes with scentless soap and for two weeks before the season he eats no meat: he is convinced that deer can identify the scent of a carnivore. "A fox runs by. That was just luck. Blacktop came along, tracking us to see where we were headed, and he passed right beneath me. I held on him, not moving, and then I let it go." The arrow passed into the rib cage just behind the shoulder, piercing the heart. "If it hadn't been for that fox, I don't think I'd've got him. I'm sure he could count. He was tracking three of us, then two of us and a fox."

The hunter's accomplishments and failures, though reported in story or demonstrated to the group in the form of the kill, are individual. The hunter is not measured against other hunters but against something more permanent and enduring. There are no famous hunters. Hunting happens beyond the city's need to generate celebrity. (Among hunters, there are a few who have achieved the status of legends. This suggests that the time-scape of hunting is that of myth rather than history.) Hunting is boring to watch because its rhythms are slow and its attraction is exercised not in physical action (though there is enough of this, in its time, to test the body: more hunters die of heart attacks than accidental gunshots) but in the state of mind and body that it evokes. "The hunter," Ortega y Gasset wrote in his *Meditations on Hunting,* "is the alert man." In this, the hunter resembles no one so much as the thinker, who must also be alive to possibilities, who must also endeavor to take nothing for granted, who also cultivates an intense and open attention because he must be prepared to catch a glimpse of the quarry in any quarter. To this I would add: if the opposite of aesthetic is anaesthetic, then I know of no more completely aesthetic activity than hunting.

My college administrator dinner companion told me that hunting as sport is wrong. Usually the people who tell me this perceive only three broad categories of human activity: work, rest, and play. And so, to his credit, the administrator was consistent: if hunting is play it is wrong, and if it is work—if one is compelled to do it for economic reasons—then it is forgivable. This is a strange kind of puritanism—strange because it leaves out another category of activity, one the puritans themselves certainly acknowledged: the ritual of holy sacrament.

I think this is the activity that hunting most closely resembles. The ritual cleansing, the mental and physical preparation, the isolation from social bonds through solitude or imposed silence—all these are prelude to the catharsis of redemption in religion and the loss of innocence in the hunt. More than one mystic has journeyed out from the city to spend forty days in the wilderness, the better to comprehend the essential qualities of being. It is no accident that in doing so they traveled beyond the land of the shepherd and ploughman to enter the landscape of the hunt, the land of predators and prey. In the terrain of the hunt a human can escape the oppressive presence of the cultural self, mirrored in the human works and tracks and trails that dominate the planet, and begin to discover what lies beneath: something prehistoric, a world devoid of human signifiers that is nevertheless alive with significance.

Hunting is undeniably sport for some. I think it shouldn't be, but am forgiving. Hunting-as-sport, you have to remember, occurs in a culture that brings us celebrity tug-of-war on television. The trophy hunter whose goal it is to accumulate experiences and stuffed heads; the profligate buffalo shooters who "hunted" from trains a hundred years ago; the urban or suburban male whose annual hunting trip offers the chance to break the bonds of culture and responsibility that define him and to be with other men in a structure of relationships relatively untainted by the rivalries of economic compulsion—all have been seduced into envisioning the hunt as sport, as ego gratification, as a distraction to fill an emptiness of time or existence, as mere negation of that which constrains and confines.

It's an attitude shaped by the necessities that impinge upon hunting in our culture. Hunting-as-sport is testimony both to our continued need to experience the primitive human nature that predates (and still underlies) the culture of the city and to the power of civil society to deflect the expression of that need, to channel it into forms that (at the least) do not subvert the premises of an actively disauthenticating culture and (at the most) might make that culture more bearable.

A chief vehicle of that deflection is language. Although hunting and farming could not be more antithetical, fish and wildlife departments across the country speak of the number of animals "harvested," speak of leaving "seed populations" in place at the end of the season, speak of game as a "renewable resource." In the world as it is, hunting as an expression of a desire for an experience with the truly other cannot attain its object. Like the farmer planting grain in amber waves, fisheries personnel stock rivers with tanker-truckfuls of beautiful, dull-witted trout. (The woods aren't stocked with deer, but only because it hasn't been necessary. Deer flourish at the edges of an agricultural landscape. There are more deer in Vermont today than when this independent country became the fourteenth state.) The Disneyfication of our world is complete. Hunters too have become consumers of experience, experiences orchestrated by a machinery that is as effectively hidden from view in the woods as the garbage trucks are hidden in tunnels beneath the Magic Kingdom.

So hunting, a practice that once defined a way of life, remains popular today as mere sport, a degraded activity, a category of activity unknown to the paleo-hunter. One of the reasons sport is popular in our culture is because the goals of our tribe include the maintenance of civil relations between strangers, which is necessary if we are to have large cities and a division of labor, and something deeply rooted within us (in all of us? or only in men?) is offended by continual and abject dependence on strangers. This is why we invent governments and then by turns mock them or use them to punish others. Under the compulsion of manners our need to experience the full panoply of our capacities is frustrated. Sport provides an arena of acceptable release. Demonstrations of physical strength, endurance, and courage outside the realm of sport or natural disaster are likely to be pathological—recall G. Gordon Liddy, holding his hand in a candle flame—unless, of course, they are channeled into war. I think it significant that war is more often described with metaphors drawn from sport than from hunting. Conflict between hunting and gathering tribes is often accepted, stylized, and therefore minimized rather than being made exceptional, ideological, and absolute.

Everyday life in a service economy doesn't test the body. Except for sport, the body's physical excellences have little outlet and so are sublimated into emotional or intellectual realms. The damage done by this abstraction can be seen anywhere a stadium full of fanatics is electrified by violence or its potential. The vicarious nature of such experience prevents the fan from achieving much of anything in the way of knowledge of self and the self's capacity for blood lust. The fan has entertained the demon and been exhilarated by it, but has been shielded from recognizing the extent to which the demon is projected from within. Hunting, even hunting-as-sport, has the virtue of offering a direct, first-person, immediate experience of culpability. In the face of that, only the most obdurate of souls can maintain an immunity to introspection.

Even so, hunters are not renowned for their sensitivity. In a common stereotype, the hunter becomes feminism's nightmare man. Prone to violence and misogyny, his annual hunting trip is a chance to drink to excess, his boisterous disregard for others hides deep insecurity, and his identification of penis with gun is a foregone conclusion. Because his willful, unapologetic commission of death is what defines him, his moral stature is nil. But this stereotype has little to do with hunting as it is and only marginally relates to hunting as it is in our society. Contrary to the agriculturalist's myth, hunting does not make the hunter bloodthirsty, does not inure the hunter to the difficulty of causing death. This, admittedly, is counterintuitive. At the risk of romanticizing the hunter, I'd go so far as to say it might even be described as mysterious.

We are so ill prepared to face mystery, and hunting presents the hunter with so many of them; is it any wonder that hunters trivialize their activity through drink and laughter? As inheritors of enlightenment rationalism we've only recently begun to see the disservice that rationalism does in trying to banish the unknowable as a category. Facing that unknowable, desirous of crediting its claim upon us, we have just a few alternatives: organized religions—agriculturalist, every one of them—which generally want no part of a ritual activity that smacks so clearly of the paganism they worked to supplant; romanticism, a tradition that negates rationalism without ever quite transcending it; and a selection of New Age healing-crystal mythologies and trendy academic irrationalisms that do encompass the possibility of mystery but are markedly inhospitable to anything so earthy and masculine as hunting. There is very little else. For the hunter seeking an idea system to explain his experience, romanticism is the best of a bad lot. And hunters aren't the only ones who see hunting through the distorting lens of romantic longing. The stereotypical image of hunter as beer-guzzling brute is as much a romantic construct as Rousseau's noble savage ever was. (There's no evidence that Jean-Jacques ever stalked his dinner.)

Ancient mapmakers sketched fanciful sea monsters and wild beasts in the margins and remote whitenesses of their world. Paleo-hunters found their solace from the mysteries of death-in-life in talisman and totem, in ritual and dance, in mimetic modes of worship and their habitation of sacred space. Until very recently the expectation in our culture has been that science will prevail, that what is and can be known is certain and measurable. We have as a consequence come to believe that in matters cognitive as well as cartographic there is little more than amusement to be gained in exercising one's urge to tell by transmuting the ineffable into faith or art. About that which we cannot speak, we must, we've been told, remain silent, and so far from being a cause to reflect on the limitations of language, or an invitation to the exercise of imagination in pursuit of capturing mystery in symbol, the great blank stretches in our knowledge (and the silence that befalls us when we find ourselves there) are, at worst, thought to be "real"—a true reflection of the nature of things—or at best a sign that (lame benediction if ever there was one) "further research is required."

But the hunter has the opportunity to know better. The hunter will know that there is a pure incipient transcendence in every movement, every stillness, every twig that crackles in the woods, for each of these foretells the moment of the archetypal event, when the hunter confronts the hunted and each becomes, in the instant, a part of the other—a psychic erasure of boundaries that has its parallel in every act of sensory perception (and yes, in the act of sexual congress). The hunt is a union of self and not-self that is ritually and literally mimicked in the act of eating that comes later, when flesh becomes flesh, when energy is transformed through death into life, when two unite as one.

Without exception the hunters I know eat what they kill, and they pause before a meal made from what they have killed in order to pay homage in one way or another to the animal that feeds them. They would no more think of foregoing this duty than they would think of treating a fast-food burger and soft drink as if they were the body and blood of Christ. To the completely rationalist mind, a meal is simply a caloric exchange—wine and bread into flesh, energy into energy, no more, no magic. I think we struggle not to be weighed down by that knowledge. We struggle, as though uphill, against a presumption that food is (simply) fuel, that nature is just stuff; we struggle to recognize in the self's incorporation of the other through eating a spiritual meaning and importance. That moment of recognition, that grace, is not impossible to achieve. I think the hunter is well placed to achieve it.

It's easy to mock the inarticulate stumblings of hunters trying to explain themselves, easy to see hunting as it is and not hunting as it could and ought to be, easy to dismiss (as Joy Williams has, in a recent essay) hunters' attempts to describe the spiritual element of their experience as being so much "intellectual blather." The hunter is as much a product of our culture as anyone else, his speech as much its captive. (Williams, too: she's ignorant of the elementary distinction between the eradication of varmints by farmers and the pursuit of game by hunters, a distinction necessary to her subject but one that popular culture doesn't offer her.) Even if we as individuals have our doubts about the ability of our culture to disenchant completely the perceptual terrain that shapes the perceiving mind, we can express our doubts most easily only as doubts, for we are that much the creatures of our creation. The positive assertion, the language of faith in the elusive, comes to modern tongues only with great difficulty. Ours is a language better suited to bullying things into understanding or compliance than to calling apparitions into being, and (a parallel) our mimetic arts have long since forsworn participatory and totemic ritual for spectacle and drama.

This means that ultimately a nonhunter's expression of distaste for what hunters are and do may be little more than a symptom of culturally evolved limitations of our language. What man, what woman, can long live outside culture? Only the sturdiest (or the most disturbed) of psyches can maintain a belief system whose categories, premises, and axiomatic truths are inexpressible in the language and experience of others. Not quite as meaningless alone as an ant or a bee, nevertheless the individual human readily displays how thoroughly the human self is a social animal. We go along to get along. When the researcher flashes a red three of clubs, we see a black three of clubs because that's what our neighbors have told us they see.

Because our language is limited, because our sociability as a species extends even to the act of perception, the tales the hunter tells—the tales that are the one universally accepted act of homage to the transcendent nature of the experience—become little more than shallow exercises in demonstrating the techniques and lore of the hunt. At their best these stories will reflect a hunter's understanding of the moral codes and perhaps even the inescapable ironies of the hunt. But self-effacing, ironic, and mocking, or grand, dramatic, even epic in the scope and telling, the stories still fall short of rendering the experience truly. An audience of hunters will know, as does the tale teller, that the action of the hunt takes place within a deeper interior terrain as well, and that the hunter has a claim to territory—a home range—like no other in this indifferent cosmos. Perhaps the story's inability to express this (and the storyteller's knowledge that imperfect though it is, the story is the only hope of expressing it) is the source of the hunter's near insatiable appetite for telling and retelling the tales. In translation, in the publicly available vocabulary of our culture, the story of any hunt is ineluctably drawn toward the corrupting presence of ego, where the knowledge shared by hunters will sound like cheap and brutal machismo. Other tribes have a vocabulary, in language and ritual and belief, that lets each tale affirm the depths of meaning of the hunt. In our tribe, mystery is reduced to mere temporary puzzlement, and the individual hunter who can't quite put into words why hunting is something other than a brutal, bloody sport is held accountable for what is, after all, a cultural ignorance.

Cartography

In the windows of an old house you can find evidence that glass is a slow and brittle liquid. Drawn by gravity, each pane gathers toward its sill, thickening perceptibly there, leaving behind a rippling wake that shapes and bends the world. Left long enough, I suppose, a window might open of its own accord, the frame emptying at the top as the glass is drawn down, freeing the room to the weather, removing one among the many layers that lie between what is and what is seen. But that would happen in geologic time. History, always and everywhere, intervenes.

In my parents' house there were many windows, each with its own interpretation of the world. From the upstairs hallway Mr. Gray's house shimmered as you walked by, as if the summer heat from his black tar driveway lasted all year. From my room, where my bed trundled under Carl's during the daytime, the clapboards on the widow Carrow's house ballooned and shrank when you moved your head, their purposeful horizontals lost to the window's slow molecular shuffle. But the strangest window, the one my brother Carl and I were most interested in, was the one next to the kitchen table. In one of its small panes was a bubble, a bottle-bottom lens that captured the whole of our backyard, from the dogwood tree in front of the barn all the way down to the hill that overlooked a curve in the Chesapeake and Delaware Canal. Carl and I fought over who got to sit next to that window until my mother commanded that we take turns.

One warm Saturday in April, in what must have been about my tenth year, it was my turn to sit by the window at breakfast. I was experimentally closing one eye and then the other, making the dogwood tree appear upside-down and far away, then right-side-up and full size, when my father entered the kitchen.

"The bathroom sink is fixed," he announced from the doorway. He shook his head at the teapot-shaped kitchen clock. "Ten o'clock already. Hoo boy! Where does the time go?"

"You really should eat something, Charles," my mother replied, standing in front of the refrigerator with an apple in each hand. "Aren't you hungry?"

"No, no, I'm fine. Maybe just a piece of toast. Where's that toast from yesterday? You didn't throw it out, did you?" He tucked his toolbox under the sideboard, pushing aside the extension cords and bags of nails that had fetched up there from some other chore, and took a seat next to me.

"I can make the cat be upside down," I told him, "and as small as a mouse."

"So what?" Carl muttered. "So can I when it's my turn."

My father didn't notice. He took an old newspaper from the pile on the chair next to him and started reading. "No, no, just like that," he said to my mother, stopping her at the toaster. "I'll take it like that. We got any marmalade?" My mother went to the refrigerator. "And some milk for the coffee."

"You should say please," I informed my father.

"Hmmm? What?" He looked up from his paper.

"You should say please when you ask for things. That's what Mommy says."

"Oh, she does, does she? Rue?" He turned an eye on my mother.

"I've been working on manners with them, Charles. Really." On the counter she laid out slices of bread in pairs, then covered half of each pair with pink tongues of luncheon meat.

My father rattled the knife in the marmalade jar, peering inside. "'Please' and 'thank you' are good for children to say," he allowed, spreading the marmalade, "but grown-ups don't have to be so formal. Right, Ruth?" He licked his fingers.

I kicked Carl under the table, trying to get him to pay attention. "Hey!" he said. "Stop that!"

"Say please," I hissed at him, "or I don't have to."

"Boys," my mother warned us. "What's the trouble?"

"Nothing," I said.

Carl looked at me carefully, then at our father, who did not look up from his paper. "Nothing," he said.

My mother sighed. "Okay," she said. "Your lunches are ready." She held up two identical paper bags, one with my name printed on it in blue crayon, one with Carl's. "Be back about midafternoon, okay?"

In Carl's fifth-grade geography book there was a picture we had studied, an artist's rendition of the brothers Columbus. Christopher held his captain's glass while Bartolomew clutched his maps. In my fourth-grade classroom I would daydream, looking out the window, imagining that we too would have such a portrait someday, Carl and I, and that Mrs. Shevock would speak of us in reverent tones, commanding the attention even of the boys in the back corner, the older ones who had flunked, the ones who sometimes pushed me around at recess. With our example before them—and with Mrs. Shevock's help—they'd be made to understand that accomplishment in the world wasn't necessarily beyond their meager grasp. If only they could know, I remember thinking, how generous I was being, how forgiving. Such was the nature of my patrimony. Unlike my mother, I hadn't produced an audience, and therefore had to settle for casting my schoolmates in that role, knowing they would need the benefit of historical distance. It comforted me to think that the world hadn't appreciated the Columbuses, either, until Christopher's voyages vindicated them both.

On the porch I paused to cinch my boots, pushing the curved enameled hook through the ladderlike placket, choosing the slots closest to the rubberized fabric so that when I levered the hook over and clicked it down, my boots would be as tight as I could get them. "Let's go," Carl said. He waited by the dogwood—a tree our Sunday school teacher told us had refused to grow tall ever since its wood had been used to make the cross. "You should have done that inside," Carl said.

"All right, all right," I said. "I'm coming."

We always had a clear purpose in mind when we undertook our explorations. That day, we were in search of an island. Neither of us had ever seen it. It rose from the marsh, held together by the roots of a few sturdy monkey-ball trees, a small oasis of solid ground in a sea of marsh grass and ooze that would suck at our feet, releasing its gassy smell with every step we took.

Carl and I first started looking for the island the summer we came to live near the marsh, when the other boys in town were slow to befriend us. We had, then, the child's awe for the power of material things, and I can still see how I first imagined the island when Carl told me about it: it was filled with bicycles, he said, and I saw machines that shone blue and red and black in the heat of the sun, their spokes a blinding wash of chrome above which swam the assorted particulars of seats and handlebars and mirrors and horns and bells. The bikes were new, not like the ones we had, embarrassingly battered and heavy, with balloon tires prone to flats and loose fenders and spokes that my father had painted with aluminum paint the day after Christmas three years before. Only Freddie Tate, the boy whose house on stilts near the edge of the marsh was barely distinguishable from the windowless chicken coop hard by it, and whose clothes always smelled of sawn wood and kerosene, had a bike that was worse than ours. The teenage boys in town mocked Freddie, and no one ever let him play with them.

Carl and I thought that Freddie's status was determined by the condition of his bike. Although it was clear to us that in the delicate

economy of camaraderie in town we stood above Freddie (he, for
one, was always willing to play with us), we also sensed that this
rank was provisional, and we wanted to firm it up.

Children, no less than adults, have a need to discern a causal
order in the world. In this they, like their elders, are easily seduced
by drama. And so when my grandmother, who usually took supper
in her room because her arthritis made the stairs impossible, appeared at table one night and announced to my father that she
would, by God, buy us new bikes if he wouldn't, we knew that once
the commotion was over our social acceptance would be assured.
Our grandmother did not make idle threats. But even without a
clear vision of cause and effect in the world, I understood its operation on my brother's imagination: while Carl held our power over
the island so naturally that I was never led to question his vision, or
even fully to realize the fact that it was his to exercise as he chose,
still I knew from the moment of my grandmother's announcement
that he and I had to have been wrong about the island. The solace
it would offer us was not what we had thought.

Carl and I had gotten close to the island the week before when
fear of deep water had made us turn back. But that day we had a
plan: we were going to build a raft. At first we thought to follow the
example suggested by the story of Moses and make a floating basket
out of marsh grass, which looked just like what the Sunday school
picture books were calling bulrushes. But Moses had been a baby,
and we were grown boys, so we would need a proportionately larger
vessel. On the whole it seemed better to follow the more realistic
example set by Huckleberry Finn. The woods around the marsh
had plenty of fallen logs, and I carried, hidden in the pouch of my
sweatshirt, my mother's clothesline. We would lash the logs together and cut the extra rope with the steak knife Carl had hidden
in his sweatshirt. We would be in business in no time.

As we walked down our sloping backyard, hands thrust into the
pouches of our matching red sweatshirts, I crinkled the top of my
lunch bag with one hand and fingered my borrowed equipment
with the other. Carl and I were careful not to look back. We didn't

speak. Once we had reached the path to the canal road and begun threading down it single file through the marsh reeds and cattails that rose above us on both sides, we breathed more easily.

"Stop a second!" Carl called, before we had gone ten feet. He froze and held a hand out, down and back—the sign we used when there were Indians ahead.

"Why?" I wanted to know. I was still feeling the moral tug of home on my soul, and the clothesline bulged large against my stomach. Our house was in plain view, its western gable still visible through the rising bulrushes that walled the path. I shifted the clothesline in my sweatshirt pouch, shielding it with my body, in case a stray parent should glance out a window.

"I heard something."

I tiptoed next to him and listened. Carl withdrew his foot and then, cautiously, returned it to where it had been. He put his weight on it, testing, and we heard a squeaking, muffled but distinct. We looked at each other as he did it again, more quickly this time. He did it again and again, and each time we heard the squeak.

"This could be it," he whispered. "The trap door!"

"Yeah! To where?"

"The other world," he hissed. "No, no, the island!"

I dropped to my knees and began prodding around Carl's foot. Then we both were looking, sorting through the papery tubes of crushed marsh weeds for a clue, a sign. Beneath the reeds his foot had been on, we found a bulbous root. "Do you think that's it?" I asked, my voice still hushed.

"Let's push it and see." Carl leaned on the root with his hand, and as it sank in the soft earth we heard the squeaking above us. We both turned our heads and saw it at the same time: a wattle of leaves and marsh reeds and twigs suspended in a bush just off the path. The bush swayed gently when Carl pushed the root.

"What is it?"

"A nest," Carl said, rising slowly. "Let's see."

Carl lifted up some twigs that made a sort of cover for the nest. Inside were five or six pink animals, each no larger than a ten-year-old's little finger. They had large heads, tiny claws, and skin that was wrinkled and wet and delicate, like the membrane under the shell of an Easter egg.

"What are they?" I asked. "They look like rabbits."

"Or skunks."

"But they're in a nest. Maybe they're birds."

"No wings. They could be possums."

"They're not snakes. They have feet."

"Right," Carl said. "Maybe squirrels."

"Let's take them home and find out."

"No!" He stopped my hand before I could touch them. "Their mothers would miss them." His voice was grave and slow—the voice, adults had impressed upon us, appropriate to solemn truths. "If we touch them, the mothers will never love them again." As we watched the animals stirred, and through their translucent skin I thought I could see each vein and muscle and organ in their bodies. I didn't dare to breathe. I moved my head closer, my eyes drawing me down to the nest, not wanting even the thinness of air to come between us.

"Let me cover them up," Carl said, pulling me back.

At that age the world before us was large and untroubled, and in it my brother and I came to know all the rabbit warrens, all the musk-rat houses, all the woodpecker trees within the compass of an after-noon's walk of our house. What my brother and I didn't know— what we could not see in our travels up and down the marshy banks of the canal (a pastime which, in memory, collapses into one long Huck Finnish idyll) was the exact apportionment being described in our lives between ignorance, which we struggled in our way to retain, and circumstance, over which we had no influence whatso-ever. This is as it should be. We were, after all, children. But as I look back on that childhood, it seems to me that a nostalgia that hasn't submitted to this discipline is likely to corrupt. It cannot es-cape the cloying pull of the merely sentimental. And once this mea-sure has been found, once you understand that childish innocence isn't anything like a gift of grace but is temporary, the product of frail inexperience, what comfort can there be in the yearning?

One day we found the carcass of a cow that had become stuck in the mud of the marsh. We checked back periodically until it was nothing but bones, whereupon we took the skull home as a trophy. The cow belonged to Mr. Biggs, an absentee farmer who was rumored to use airplanes to catch trespassers, and who owned most of the land to the east of town. His pastures lined the canal, rising above the bulrushes of the canal-side marshes, separated from them by steep wooded banks that wound around the marsh's infinite fingers and coves. Here, where the cows came to drink, was a terrain as compelling as the marsh. I couldn't have explained it then, but what drew me to it was its unlikely collision of elements, the rolling fields, the steep and wooded hillsides, the flat expanse of the meandering marsh threaded through with a network of creeks and rivulets that swelled to fullness on the tide.

Carl and I made it our project to map the wanderings of the shoreline, filling in details—the Cow Hole here, the Tree Root Cavern there—believing that when everything had been recorded and named, what was left would be our island. Every airplane that passed overhead brought with it fear of discovery and we would scurry to hide ourselves from view, supremely unaware of how insignificant we would have been within the wide horizons that stretched out beneath the pilot. We knew from saying the Lord's Prayer that trespassing was a serious offense, one that required the intervention of God Himself to set to rights—and we hoped that as long as our purpose remained focused on the island, He would have to take our side against anybody, even Mr. Biggs.

I've long since lost that map. The terrain it recorded is gone as well, buried now under dredging spoils, tier upon tier of gray mud that dried to dust, put there by the Army Corps of Engineers when they widened and deepened and straightened the canal. A hundred years ago, the town must have welcomed the commerce and activity that the canal brought to it. Pictures show the canal to have been a small thing then, barely wider than the horse-drawn barges it accommodated. There were locks at the foot of our street. Later pictures show excursion steamers bringing visitors from Wilmington and Philadelphia, men in top hats and ladies in bonnets and full skirts looking festive while they wait for the locks to fill. Mr. Gray, who was a young man then, loaded sacks of grain at the wharf, and others made their livings at concessions catering to that elegant trade. But successive dredgings and widenings ate the heart out of the town, its buildings and streets counting as nothing against the forces that wanted a deep-draft passage between Philadelphia and Baltimore. "By their works shall you know them": the army's purpose had always been larger than the development of our transportation infrastructure, though the burden they carried for all of us, the burden of redeeming culture through the energetic reformation of a profane, inefficient nature, was mostly left unstated.

The embankments they produced near my childhood home have a geometric precision. It would take only a moment to sketch them out, and there is no room along them for the island we hoped to find. Where once Carl and I could lose ourselves enough to become disoriented, and so come upon the canal by surprise, spotting the masts and booms of a cargo ship as they moved silently through the woods, there is now only a flat and open plain, as spare and forbidding as the rules my father gave to all of us in that house.

There is something in human nature that is violated by such simplicity, however much we think we want it. At night, before I fell asleep, I would latch my fingers into the springs under Carl's bed and pull my bed back under his. I had to do it slowly. If my father heard the wheels squeak, he would come up and pull the bed out again, telling me I couldn't breathe. My mother let me stay under there. With Carl's bed above me, and his bedclothes hanging down around me, I was safe. I could hardly hear the voices from downstairs. I could only hear Carl, whose voice was clear and soft when he answered my questions through the mattress.

One night after we had been exploring and had almost been spotted by an airplane, I asked him if Mr. Biggs had anything to do with God. I think I had detected a continuity of judgment in my life, a direct line of observation that proceeded from my father, through Mr. Biggs and Santa Claus, on up to God, whose qualities—omniscience, omnipresence, infallibility—trickled down in decreasing measure to the others.

"You should ask Mrs. McNatt tomorrow," Carl said. She was our Sunday school teacher, a southern Delawarean whose commitment to Plessy versus Ferguson extended even to the hereafter. When Prince died, she told me I wouldn't ever see him again because dogs had their own separate and equal heaven, "just like the Negroes."

"What do you think he'd do if we found the island?"

"Who?"

"Mr. Biggs."

"I don't know," Carl said. "Go to sleep."

"I can't." My father's voice was the one that was hardest to hear. It didn't carry at all, because he didn't raise it, ever. The neighbors would only hear my mother, hysterical. Under Carl's bed, late at night, protected from the world, I practiced the art of inference until the sounds downstairs made sense.

"I know," Carl told me.

A few years later, just before Christmas, my eighth-grade English teacher would assign "The Gift of the Magi," struggle hard to get us to comprehend the idea of irony, and fail. Our obduracy was appropriate. It is, after all, cruel to steal from children. And yet Mrs. Flynn would have succeeded had she told me that I already understood: that in the marshes along the canal I'd already experienced what I so dutifully tried to describe to her in terms of lockets of hair and pocket watches. Let me speak with adult hindsight, more clearly than I ever spoke to Mrs. Flynn. The mistake I made with O. Henry was to think that irony has a necessary connection to will, that its essence is found in some perversion of causality, and that therefore I, with my desires inarticulate and bound up within me, could remain immune to it. I was ignorant of the possibilities afforded by accident and happenstance, the stuff of history, pure and simple.

This, at any rate, is what befell my brother and me on our way to find our island. After Carl pulled me away from the nest that day I felt a need to assert myself. "We have to change the name," I told him as he covered up the nest. "Now it's 'Nest-of-Babies Place.'"

"Okay, but I get to write it down, because you thought it up."

Carl and I continued down the path toward the canal, being careful not to knock down any new marsh reeds so that the path would remain narrow and tight. We had just set foot on the yellow sandy dirt of the road when we were brought up short. There, next to the path, was a red convertible. Slowly we walked around the back of it, admiring the slice of its fins, the bright shine of its bumper.

On the other side of the car a pair of legs protruded from underneath and a man squatted next to them, smoking. He wore old dungarees, a cowboy hat, pointy boots. "Hey!" he said. "Where'd you come from?"

"Up there," Carl said, pointing up the hill toward our backyard. "What's the matter? Did your car break?"

"Who you talkin' to?" came a voice from under the car.

"Two kids," said the man, flicking his cigarette into the marsh weed.

"That might start a fire," Carl informed him.

The legs wiggled, becoming slowly longer, until they joined a torso. A grimy face appeared near the rear wheel. "No, our car didn't just break," it said. "It got broken."

"How?" my brother asked.

"Two boys did it," the man answered. He swiped at his cheek with the back of a greasy hand, rubbing the dirt deeper into the stubble on his face, and squinted at us. "Two boys in red sweatshirts. Looked just like you."

"Let's get out of here," I whispered, tugging on Carl's sweatshirt.

"Try that now, Hank," said the face under the car, and the man got up and slid onto the seat behind the wheel.

I used his inattention to make my escape. I broke and started running down the canal road, running as hard as I could. Carl followed. I held my lunch like a football, sucked in deep breaths, and ran until the road curved up a small rise and around a bend where, out of sight, I felt safe. I collapsed at the foot of a tree that shaded the road. Carl leaned on his knees and panted.

"What are we going to do?" I asked him.

"About what?"

"They're going to get us for breaking that car."

"We didn't break that car," Carl pointed out.

"I know, I know, but we can't prove it. You heard him. He said they had red sweatshirts, just like ours." I wished with all my heart that my mother had gotten the blue sweatshirts, the ones we almost bought, instead. I was close to tears, thinking that this one small arbitrary choice of hers was going to send us to reform school for the rest of our lives.

"C'mon," my brother said. "They were just teasing us. They know we didn't break their car."

"You really think so?"

"Yes."

"How do you know?"

"I just know."

I was mollified, but not totally convinced. I felt the tears recede.

"Let's go find a place to have lunch," Carl said.

Memory is a notorious compressor, which I take to be evidence not only that humans are prone to false and convenient witness but that the urge to make art is deeply rooted, even unconscious, within us. And such compression, whereby the distance between important things is reduced, bringing them into useful relation, is, after all, the whole point of a map. I say this because it is possible that in my memory of that day I have shaped myself a lesson. At any rate, as I recall it, Carl and I walked along the canal road until we came to a culvert, one that let the ditch on our left empty into the canal. There the marsh extended farther from the road than we had ever been able to go. Freddie told us he walked through it once, duck hunting with his father, but we didn't believe him. No one had ever gone all the way in there and come out again. On our map it remained a blank white spot. We climbed down off the road into the ditch, jumped the small water that ran in its bottom, and used the roots of the marsh reeds to pull ourselves up the sloping brown mud of the bank. After matting down the reeds to make a seat, we started eating our sandwiches.

I had a hard time with mine. I had a lump in my throat from my near brush with injustice and could hardly swallow. I knew, from watching *Highway Patrol* and *Perry Mason* in the afternoons with my grandmother in her room, the difficulty with which truth was established in court. I trusted Carl, but knew that there were vast stretches of my life for which I had no alibi. If those two men happened to tell the police that their car had been broken during one of those times, I knew that I would be in a great deal of trouble. Who would believe two kids as against two grownups?

Carl finished his sandwich and put the balled-up waxed paper back into his bag. He fished around in the bag until he found the apple at the bottom, and then, lying back on the crushed marsh weeds in the warm sun, one hand behind his head and his knees in the air, he took a bite of it. "You know," he said, "we don't have to look for the island today."

"I know."

"Do you want to?"

"No." I found my apple and began eating it.

"Do you want to get some monkey balls and throw them in the canal?"

"No."

"Me neither."

When I was done with my apple, I threw the core as far as I could into the canal, knowing that it would float for a while before a fish bobbed up to eat it. I slid down into the ditch and stuck my hand in the mud of the bank. It was warm and thick and familiar. As I squeezed it through my fingers I could see silvery flecks of some mineral spread throughout the mud.

I took another handful and plopped it into the stream, then another, and then another. Soon Carl joined me. Without actually agreeing on it, we had decided to abandon forever the search for our island; I think we knew, then, that it simply didn't exist. And what did we do? Like model engineers, we built dams and sluices for the stream, taking warm handfuls of mud and mixing in straw and twigs to give it form. Carl found a thistle and cut little pieces from it with the steak knife to make trees for a forest. We imported sand from the canal road and gave our river a bed, underscoring its entire length in yellow. It was a technical marvel. It was beautiful.

As we worked we stirred up silt, and over and over again it pleased me enormously to watch our river clean itself and run pure, as clear as glass, right before our eyes.

The Rootless Professors

Shortly after I moved to Vermont to teach I was gassing up at Dudley's—a local general store, the sort of eclectic commercial institution for which Vermont is justly renowned—when I overheard a conversation that I marked as peculiar. One young man was admiring another's car, allowing that he had once owned one like it.

"So," the car owner said, "you from around here?"

"No," came the reply. "I'm from North Montpelier."

I thought this strange, because the place where we stood was only two miles from the village of North Montpelier.

At the time I thought I had overheard a classic instance of the parochialism of rural life. I certainly wouldn't have answered the question that way. I tend to say that I'm from "around here" if I'm anywhere within twenty miles of where I regularly sleep. But as I thought about that exchange it struck me as something else: a manifestation of a geographical sensibility very different from my own, a sensibility whose deeply buried, unexamined notions of territory, home range, and locale have some distinct advantages over the cosmopolitanism that I was trained to as an academic.

As citizens of the *cosmo polis,* the mythical "world city," academics are expected to owe no allegiance to geographical territory. They're supposed to belong to the boundless world of books and ideas and eternal truths, not the infinitely particular world of watersheds, growing seasons, and ecological niches. Most academics get their jobs through national searches, and while an individual professor might have a preference for a specific region of the country, most who found jobs after the boom years of the sixties are living wherever they could find work. Other professions, too, have national markets for their services and so have an economically driven rootlessness, but academics seem an extreme case. The extremity results from the fineness of focus of academic specialization and the limited utility of their services. Typically a town of twenty thousand will support a clutch of lawyers, doctors, schoolteachers, or accountants, but it's a rare and generally only a much larger, urban ecosystem that will have a niche for more than one teacher of, say, the literature of medieval Italy.

Like everyone else, academics tend to turn necessity into virtue. The ethos of rootlessness is so strong in academe that I suspect the experience of an acquaintance of mine is exceptional only for the bluntness with which the message was conveyed: having gotten his degrees from the university in the state where he was born, and having worked at that institution for a few years as a lecturer on a semester-by-semester appointment, he was told flatly (though unofficially) by the chair of his department that he was "too much a native" ever to become a permanent faculty member.

The majority of American college students attend institutions in their home states, where they are taught, by and large, by members of an exotic and transient class. I suspect the values and general outlook of these rootless professors influence the values and general outlook of their charges, the students who survive their tutelage to become the best-informed, best-educated part of the American public. I suspect that because they are themselves unrooted, the cosmopolitan professoriat tends to think "disconnected from locale" is a necessary part of "educated." Historically their practice has at times consisted of little more than an organized assault on the parochial point of view, the view of the rooted "I." Education can be that. Education certainly ought to broaden one's horizons, but it can and should do more. However we define that "more," one thing seems clear: because professors tend to be rootless, they are systematically denied experience of one key element of an integrated life—the life that is, after all, one of the primary goals of a liberal arts education. They are woefully ignorant of the value to be found in being connected to place.

As are, of course, most of their charges: rootlessness is now the norm, the usual condition. A cosmopolitan professor can hardly expect to awaken students from dogmatic slumbers by confirming them intellectually in an attitude most have willingly adopted since they first could tune in to MTV and cruise the local mall. Throughout the academy there are so few examples of postadolescent youth being stunted in their intellectual development by constraining bonds of kinship, community, and family history that the old battle cry of cosmopolitan antiparochialism now rings hollow, as hollow as any other call to fight a long-vanquished foe. It's time to examine this cosmopolitanism and to reckon its consequences.

The most obvious consequence of the trained rootlessness of the academic class is our culture's superficial, exploitative, ignorant relationship to nature. It takes a college education to move into just about any position of responsibility in the modern economy. From the standpoint of the spotted owl or the eastern catamount or any of the dozens of amphibious species that seem to be disappearing from our world, the typical college education looks like nothing so much as the consummatory moment in a complex reproductive cycle, a nonsexual exchange of nongenetic information that perpetuates the ecologically oblivious human as a type. A rootless class is likely to see nature as so much visual furniture—a barely differentiated backdrop to the important activities of their lives, the land you drive through or fly over to get where you're going, a collation of scenery that may charm or console or amuse as it unfurls. How many college teachers (excluding, say, hydrologists and geographers) can describe the watershed in which they live? My limited and admittedly unscientific sampling suggests the answer: very few. Water is absolutely necessary to life—ninety-some percent of the body is water—yet most academics have no idea whence theirs comes or where it goes when its incorporative service is done.

You don't need to be a follower of Thales, ready to find metaphysical or spiritual meaning in water, to see this as significant. Knowing where your water comes from and where your sewage goes is a basic element of citizenship in an ecosystem. The academic's learned ignorance, the academic's belief that this is a *worthy* ignorance—the tacit belief that such things as watersheds are parochial details, transcended by the grand synthetic truths of cosmopolitan training—is a significant root of our culture's ongoing environmental crisis. For decades our best and brightest planners and policymakers have been taught to view nature as inert, scarcely differentiated, infinitely manipulatable "stuff." By training, by historical tradition, by uncritical acceptance of a philosophical tradition that dates back to Descartes, and by virtue of a conspicuous lack in their education, they dismissed knowledge of what lay before them as unimportant. No one taught them the capacity to appreciate the specific genius of place. No one *could* teach them, because none of their teachers knew.

The effect of academic rootlessness on our culture's political psyche is less obvious but I think no less real. It contributes to a shallow and emotional nationalism, a dangerous political passion that is too much in evidence in our public life and on our campuses. Any educator worthy of the name is discouraged by unthinking jingoism, of whatever political stripe. It's especially discouraging to see that jingoism as being in part the product of education. But I think that this is so.

In renouncing or at best minimizing their citizenship in the political, biotic, and familial communities of their homes and embracing citizenship in the world city of ideas and culture, our rootless professors set an example for young citizens: this is what it means to be smart, to be educated. Cultivate the big picture, their example says, and break free of narrow, claustrophobic horizons. Students thus learn to give up real and immediate connections to things concretely observable in favor of a less immanent, less obvious, less emotionally satisfying connection to abstraction. The cosmopolitan ideal, either more or less explicit in the curriculum, is a global community of scholarship and symbol making.

But that community proves a bit too abstract for some, perhaps most students. Their emotional need to belong isn't satisfied by membership in a world that is neither corporally nor temporally present, a world in which most of them can only be spectators, never full participants, a world which has no mechanism by which to acknowledge their membership (or even their simple presence). These are shortcomings that the nation-state is careful to avoid. With its flags and heroes and simple villains, with its equality of participation, its reductive Manichean morality and its call to the easy sacrifices of an altruism based thoroughly on an only marginally enlightened self-interest, the nation-state will always be more effectively and compellingly symbolized than the world of books and ideas and art. Membership in the nation offers immediate emotional satisfactions that life as a cosmopolite offers only after much training of the sensibilities. This helps to explain why in the past decade the most belligerent and cynical of U.S. foreign policies— the invasion of Grenada, the bombing of Libya, the invasion of Panama, the expulsion of Iraq from Kuwait—have received surprising support among college students, who as a group have been dismayingly ready to accept jingoistic slogans and patriotic appeals in lieu of moral or even practical argument. But it isn't surprising that once students have been disconnected from locale they choose the nation-state over the larger abstraction of "culture." They need to belong to something, and membership in the nation-state, the less abstract abstraction, is easy, satisfying, expected, rewarded.

Nationalism is one manifestation of what can be described as the etherealizing tendency of modern culture, a process by which the elements of life that used to provide orientation and grounding have been made progressively more distant, abstract, general, and ultimately less than fully satisfying. Over the last century and a half the bonds of family and community have been loosened and have been replaced (when they've been replaced at all) with voluntary affiliations based on nation, on the abstract categories of identity politics, or on membership in the socioeconomic ghetto of a "lifestyle enclave." Work has evolved from the physical business of manufacturing to the more abstract provision of service to the even more abstract manipulation of information and symbols. "All that is solid," Marx diagnosed, "melts into air." Our educational system and especially the professoriat as a rootless class are implicated in that process. The identification of a common core or canon, such as was done in the thirties by Robert Hutchins at Chicago, can be seen as an attempt to fight fire with fire. The Great Books Tradition—distant, abstract, homogeneous—was supposed to unify and ground a polity spun apart and unrooted by the centrifugal forces of economic change, immigration, urbanization.

It isn't exactly self-evident that dragging eighteen-year-olds toward an appreciation of cultural works by long-dead, distant Europeans will necessarily give them a footing in the world. That cosmopolitan project has in recent years come under heavy fire from champions of the marginalized cultures it excludes. I think it is time to criticize it from the vantage of a rooted education. From that perspective multicultural inclusiveness doesn't necessarily solve the problem. Reading works by members of diverse, formerly marginalized American subcultures will broaden an undergraduate's horizons (though if all across the nation students are reading the same Latina novel, the same Asian-American novel, the same gay novel, our collective cultural horizon isn't broadened as much as it might be). But by its nature multiculturalism tends to perpetuate a pedagogy of placeless identity rather than a pedagogy of rootedness in place. Identity politics, it seems, is the continuation of cosmopolitanism by other means. "The race," "the folk," "the ethnic group," "the sexual-orientation minority" are abstractions as ethereal as "educated people everywhere," "the western tradition," or "the nation."

What we lack is rooted community. While we argue about what version of abstraction might best serve in its absence, beyond the campus gate lie the last vestiges of an indigenous regional culture, a unique adaptation of belief and practice to geographic place that is slowly evolving itself out of existence as the forces of cultural homogenization work their way on it. Yes, the classics of western (or any) culture have something to teach us about being human, for they transcend the limits of historical and geographical origin in their beauty and meaning. But how can a student appreciate this quality without being able to appreciate how those works are also rooted in the particularness of the place and time of their creation? And how can students appreciate *that* if they have no knowledge of how they themselves are tied to locale and time? Experience of regional culture, of the systems of meaning that people have created that do not aspire to a kind of placeless universality, would provide a needed complement, a necessary rooting. Such an experience would bring universality into focus through contrast rather than by default. But as a rootless, cosmopolitan class, professors are generally disinclined and usually unfit to give students such experience. Education—and through it, the national character—is the shallower for this lack.

I don't mean to deny the virtues of cosmopolitanism. The rootlessness of professors has helped to guarantee that postsecondary education will not be captive to local concerns and perspectives, or overly subject to the tyranny of state legislatures, or overly restricted in its presentation of ideas, beliefs, and exemplars of life choices and ways of being. The national market for college teachers has helped us avoid prejudice and pettiness and narrowness of thinking in academe. It has been an effective device for spreading alternative and unconventional schools of thought, and all of that is healthy.

But to the extent that the professorial class is a carrier of culture, the national market for academic services (along with the modern communications and transportation systems that make that market possible) has contributed to the homogenization of culture in our nation.

Examples aren't hard to find. One winter morning in 1980 when I ducked into a general store to buy a cup of coffee on the way to work, I had to wait at the register behind an old man who bought ten pounds of potatoes, thirty pounds of flour, a brick of lard, four sets of bootlaces, and a section of stovepipe. He had ventured out of his house to do a monthly restocking, like some character from a Laura Ingalls Wilder novel. No one shops that way now. No one *can* shop that way in Vermont anymore, because a new generation of general store owners with mortgage payments to make has transformed the typical general store into a clapboard-sided minimart stocking bread, milk, soda, beer, videos, chips, and not much else. The old nuts-and-bolts, stovepipe, hardware-and-flannel-shirt inventory didn't move, and so it's gone.

With the change we've lost that old man's orientation in time, his sense of home as a winter fastness, his sense of the local store as both the focus of public life and an avenue of exchange with the larger world. His mentality is no longer a part of our collective consciousness. Without it, Vermont becomes incrementally more like Anywhere. Every part of our country is now less different from every other part than it was even twenty years ago. Loss of diversity— even if difference was sometimes manifest as benighted and oppressive belief—can never be wholly good.

At issue, ultimately, is a cardinal point in the western tradition, seen most clearly in the realm of epistemology, in the theories of knowledge we employ. We in the western world have traditionally valued the universal over the particular, the general statement over the local exception, the grand capital-T-truth over the particular details of the specific cases from which that truth was induced. And so the truths that our professorial class carries are supposed to be the truths that transcend time and place. How could that carriage not be a good thing?

Here is an example, by way of analogy. Sometime shortly after the near meltdown, in 1978, of a nuclear power plant at Three Mile Island outside Harrisburg, Pennsylvania, a majority of Americans polled agreed with the proposition that nuclear power is a necessary component of the nation's energy system. A majority also agreed, however, with the proposition that nuclear power is inherently unsafe, and said that they would not want a nuclear plant built near their home. This poll might be said to have caught American opinion in transition and hence in contradiction, and perhaps that's true, but I think there is something else afoot here. Both answers are reasonable. To say, "I want nuclear power, but not near me," violates no logical precept. There is, however, a moral contradiction.

In the western rootless tradition our tendency has been to credit the wishes of the majority answering the first question and to discount or dismiss the wishes of the majority responding to the second. The first question, tradition would have it, deals with the issue in its "purest," most general form, divorced from any consideration of circumstance or context. The responses to the second are infected, apparently, with narrow self-interest or (to use a phrase I have heard Marxists use) "local particularism."

The issue hasn't gone away with the decline of nuclear power. Policymakers refer to the "NIMBY syndrome," the "Not-In-My-Back-Yard!" ire that development can engender. The phrase is condescending. To say that opponents of one or another planned development suffer from "NIMBY Syndrome" is to suggest that the resistance of people with an investment in the future of the land they inhabit is a narrow, selfish resistance, rather than principled resistance—and we all agree that only principled resistance is worthy, right?

But why? To reason this way is to give preference to the voice of the abstract at the expense of the voice of the particular. This we can only do if we dismiss out of hand the possibility that because moral questions come to us not in the abstract but as concrete, particular problems, their solutions might well be particular and specific. If no single member of a political community wants a garbage dump in their backyard, by what transubstantiating magic could the community be said to want one at all? If the community doesn't want a garbage dump, perhaps it needs to be taught how not to have one, rather than be led through political exercises that will locate the dump in the least powerful, least politically astute neighborhood.

As with the moral aspects of zoning, so with epistemology and morals generally. A plea for a diversity of approaches would have us defend the possibility that particularism has something to offer, and it is just this possibility that tends to be denied by an educational system reliant on rootless professionals for its personnel.

What is to be done?

The underlying causes of the rootless professorial class aren't going to go away, and they aren't particularly amenable to dramatic alteration. The national market for academic services isn't going to disappear, not as long as scholarship is so specialized that job advertising must be national in scope, not as long as transportation is relatively cheap, not as long as the market is so tight that candidates consider themselves lucky to get a job at all, let alone one in a region they could conceivably call home. We are very far from the days when students attended the local college and the most gifted among them were recruited to serve on the faculty upon graduation.

If we can't get rid of the causes of the problem, we can at least alleviate the symptoms. And this is probably the better course—it gives us the chance to keep what is good in both cosmopolitanism and rootedness.

First, the academy needs to overcome its prejudice against the local and provincial, so that its hiring committees do not include nonnative status as an implicit qualification for employment. The acquaintance I mentioned sought a job for which he was qualified in a region whose species, seasons, and landforms he knew. That knowledge, it seems, counted against him. It shouldn't have. The diversity with which the academy aims to challenge students should include that rarest of all academics, the learned professor at home in a place.

Second, professors should take the trouble to include local content in their courses. Not abstract theories about distant peoples, but concrete realizations about observable communities; not airy generalizations that transcend student experience and lie beyond their powers of criticism, but specific conclusions whose skeptical testing they can perform themselves; not social-science hearsay taken on faith, but evidence weighed critically, firsthand: this is where a rooted education begins. If education is most successful when it renders the student's world by turns problematic and comprehensible, puzzling then scrutable, then local content will increase teaching effectiveness. Transforming the social and natural world outside the classroom into education's subject matter (and the corollary transformation of classroom experience into a brief respite from the problematic world, a respite in which tools and theories are honed) will tend to erase the artificial boundary between the roles of student and citizen. That, too, would be good. We want to encourage in the latter the habits of the former. Curious, skeptical, reasonable, taking little on faith, accustomed to carrying careful inquiry into the world, such a citizenry will more nearly fit the mold that democracy requires. And if we imagine for them also a commitment to their community—not just to the people but to the land, water, flora, and fauna of their place of habitation—that citizenry begins to resemble the kind of polity we need if industrial mass democracy is ever going to save itself from its own worst consequences.

Third, professors could take more seriously the regional branches of the professional organizations in the various disciplines, rather than seeing them as proving grounds for bright graduate students and low-level professors. If they were to serve as forums for the development of curricula rooted in locale, their work could have real meaning and importance, rather than being a political alternative to or a pale reflection of the agenda of the national organizations.

Fourth, we ought to establish a cultural expectation for ecological literacy and provide the schooling to allow citizens to achieve it. As Aldo Leopold noticed half a century ago (in the classic *A Sand County Almanac*), we teach our children how to read but not how to read a landscape for its history. While it's easy to see how textual literacy has something to do with individual quality of life, the pay-off for ecological literacy isn't so clear, so we don't require it, even though in the long run and to the species as a whole it's likely to prove equally important. All education, David Orr has written, is environmental education. If we're going to salvage the earth from the forces of unsustainability that we've loosed upon it, we need to revise dramatically the environmental curriculum we've been offering.

Finally, academics ought to work to acquire a kind of dual citizenship—in the world of ideas, yes, but also in the very real world of watersheds and growing seasons and migratory pathways and food chains and dependency webs that exist outside their classrooms. What is needed is a class of cosmopolitan educators willing to live where they work and to work where they live, a class of educators willing to take root, willing to inhabit rather than merely reside, to do the learning and walking and perceiving and the hands-on physical work necessary to cultivate a sense of place. These educators could then exemplify in their teaching and in their lives their own manner of accommodation to the irresolvable tension between the local and the universal, the particular and the general, the concrete and the abstract.

In an age when humanity's relationship to nature is so in need of careful, farsighted attention, I think this much is clear: academics do a disservice to their students, and to the future of human culture on the planet, if they do anything less.

The Contemporary Relevance of Henry Adams

I n the sunbaked fields and salt marshes around the family home in Quincy, where he summered as a boy, Henry Adams knew a freedom that was denied to him in Boston. "Summer was the multiplicity of nature," he wrote in *The Education of Henry Adams;* "winter was school." And again: "Summer was tropical license," winter "always the effort to live."

The division seems to have run deep—deep enough to suggest that within his being the contrast of seasons had found and aligned with other, congruent antinomies. From this tendency to see the world in terms of paired antagonistic forces he never escaped, not through any of his successive abandonments: of Master Tower's Trinitarian lessons, from which he graduated to the more expansive, chestnut-shaded halls of Harvard Yard; of watchful Boston, the city of his father and his accomplished ancestors, which he abandoned once for Germany and then again, later, after a stint as a professor of history at Harvard, for Washington, where he thought he and his bride might better find a circle appreciative of her caustic wit; of the life of social engagement he led with Marian Hooper Adams, as host and hostess of the closest thing to a salon the District of Columbia had ever seen, which he abandoned for life as a shy and misanthropic widower in the wake of her suicide in 1885.

We shouldn't be surprised to learn that his misanthropy might have been as much a studied pose as it was a heartfelt plaint. The complex interplay of contradictions was, he told us, the most decisive force he knew. Its form was honored in the capacity for profound ambivalence that he maintained throughout his life, an ambivalence he described at the age of twenty-four in a letter to his eldest brother, Charles, explaining why the pursuit of politics (something of a family calling) didn't hold interest for him: "To a man whose mind is balanced like mine," he wrote, "in such a way that what is evil never seems unmixed with good, and what is good always streaked with evil, an object never seems important enough to call out strong energies until they are exhausted, nor necessary enough not to allow of its failure being possible to retrieve; in short, a mind which is not strongly positive and absolute, cannot be steadily successful in action, which requires quietness and perseverance."

He wasn't fickle. By nature and disposition balanced in his attachments and provocative, even outrageous in his pronouncements, he was a sensitive and careful thinker, a pessimist, a sharp and playful intellect given to ironic distance and iconoclasm. His are virtues typical of disgruntled brilliance and, some have said, of his place as the bright, runtish middle child of an austere father. (He was the third son of Charles Francis Adams, that son of John Quincy and grandson of John, and his stature in life was affected by a childhood bout of scarlet fever; short, a shade under five feet four, he had a carpenter shorten the legs of the furniture in the house he built in Washington, so his feet could reach the floor.) Not fickleness but deep ambivalence cradled his discontent—ambivalence, that perverse and contradictory spur, felt most keenly by those with an excellent imagination and a complex, empathic vision.

Adams's life encompassed America's growth as a nation and its rise to international power. He came of age in the years just before the American Civil War (again that sense of warring opposites), which he spent in London, serving his father (the American ambassador to England) as private secretary, and he lived to see the start of World War I. From his house on Lafayette Square in Washington, he kept a sometimes amused and always wary eye on the successive occupants of the White House. Having written a definitive history of the United States covering the first sixteen years of the nineteenth century (a history that took almost as long in the chronicling as in the occurrence and that won a prize he refused to accept), in the 1890s he turned his considerable powers of comprehension to the future, reading as perceptively as anyone the course that would be traced by that oxymoronic political form, that American dynamo, mass democracy, as it assumed its mature industrial, imperial form.

The errors of the late nineteenth century were many, and prominent among them was the tone of absolute certainty in its self-congratulation. Sometimes Adams was led by his sense of compensatory balance to an extremity of scorn for its accomplishments. He mocked the lockstep march of progress and the dogmas of national power, becoming a modern Luther not so much posting theses as loitering near the doorway, sardonically surveying those who sought communion in the most popular church of the era. "When I happened to fall in with him on the street he could be delightful," a neighbor, Oliver Wendell Holmes, wrote of the aged Adams; "but when I called at his house and he was posing to himself as the old cardinal he would turn everything to dust and ashes." ("After a tiresome day's work," Holmes went on, somewhat apologetically, "one didn't care to have one's powers of resistance taxed by discourse of that sort, so I called rarely.")

T. S. Eliot, explaining in a review of the *Education* Adams's professed failure to achieve any knowledge worthy of the name, said that education is a by-product of "being interested, passionately absorbed," and that Adams showed "extreme sensitiveness to all the suggestions that dampen enthusiasm or dispel conviction." Yes: conviction is a form of single-mindedness, and Adams seemed incapable of that. Yet he didn't lack passion—for his work, certainly (you don't work for ten years on a nine-volume history without mustering some capacity for passionate absorption), and most especially for his wife, Marian (known universally as Clover), whose suicide inaugurated what he called his "posthumous existence." In most everything else he was so thoroughly ambivalent that he was even a lukewarm doubter, a paradoxically credulous skeptic. Wanting solace after Clover's death he flirted for a time with Buddhism. In Ceylon, on a world trip with his friend LaFarge, he journeyed by oxcart to Anuradhapura to sit under the sacred Bo—a scion cultured from the very tree that shaded the Buddha during his apotheosis. ("A sickly shoot," he reported to Lizzie Cameron; after sitting under it for half an hour, he left "without attaining Buddhaship.")

Later he wrote respectful but essentially agnostic poetry to the Virgin of Chartres. He came so to appreciate the emotional power that her worship held for others that he undertook to seek its origin and produced one of the finest works ever written about medieval cathedrals, the classic *Mont-Saint-Michel and Chartres*.

It is a masterwork, this short volume on two cathedrals. Published privately for "the amusement of a few friends" (as were most of his writings after *The History of the United States during the Administrations of Thomas Jefferson and James Madison*), the volume presents Adams as he would most like to be remembered: as a learned and genial uncle, enlightening his "nieces-in-wish" during a leisurely autumn tour of the French countryside. In it we feel his envy for a time when the world was unified and ennobled by its celebration of the Virgin and for the unselfconscious wholeness brought by the grace she generously offered. The foundation of Adams's continuing claim on our attention is to be found in this book and in its companion volume, the pseudoautobiographical *Education of Henry Adams*.

The two are strikingly different. The first is a work of architectural appreciation that ranges over an incredible breadth of ground as it grapples with its central problem: why are these two cathedrals, built scarcely a hundred years apart, so different in design and affect? Adams brings to bear a commanding knowledge of the technical, historical, literary, theological, and cultural factors that shaped medieval stone, and he does so in a voice that is at once avuncular, learned, and enthusiastic. In the second work Adams speaks in the third person, dissecting his life, giving a dispassionate and melancholy account of his course through the nineteenth century, professing failure and exuding world-weariness at every turn. The book's narrator, says one critic, is "a tired old man who knows too much about life to find it worth living."

In this doubling, in the distance Adams measures with these two opposites, lies what we need to know.

Different as the two works are, they need to be understood together. It's best to take Adams at his word when he tells us, in the *Education,* that they were conceived as parts of a single project. That project had its efficient cause in the Crisis Summer of 1893, in a visit Adams made to his younger brother, Brooks, at the family home in Quincy.

In 1893 Adams had been a widower for eight years and three years previously had completed his *History,* that work whose composition had formed his own escape from the world that Clover abandoned. In 1886, the year after Clover's suicide, he had traveled to Japan (where he regained his grief-suppressed sense of smell) with the painter John LaFarge. A few years later, in 1890, he had journeyed again to the Far East with LaFarge, on the round-the-world jaunt he undertook when the completion of his *History* left him feeling Clover's absence too keenly. He arrived back in Washington in 1892 with a taste for travel—he would, from then on, spend a good portion of each year abroad—and with doubts about the historical method he had used in the *History.*

In the nine volumes of that work he had aimed to provide only enough narrative to thread his documentary sources together. His intention had been (as he once advised an amateur historian who wrote to him) to "let the documents speak for themselves." After his journey he understood that this was not the sum total of the historian's role. On the island of Tahiti he had immersed himself in new researches—his depression was manifest as boredom, and years of proper Bostonian habit prescribed work as the cure for ennui. In the resulting history (a complex tale of the island's genealogies, presented as the first-person memoirs of Marau Taaroa, the queen of Tahiti, and made poignant by the fact that western contact brought western concepts of land ownership; the division of the tropical commons into hereditary claims made genealogy a matter of pressing legal interest) the method of his major work is reversed: the emphasis in the queen's history is on narrative, not on evidence and facticity. Indeed, Adams's queen speaks eloquently, from a familiarity with western culture and history that would have been beyond her necessarily limited experience. In her memoirs Adams was exploring the median between history and fiction. By the Crisis Summer of 1893 Adams had come to understand the need for historical integument, for a matrix or context that alone could bring facts (which he now saw as ambiguous) into meaningful relation.

To say that Clover's death marked a turning point in Adams's life is understatement. Adams felt himself wrenched in two, and if her death didn't create it certainly intensified his feeling that the world lacked a unifying power, that it was not, as it might appear, a frustrating albeit orderly place but was something else, something more formidable and chilling. Undifferentiated, wholly indifferent, it was no universe at all, not a unified anything but a multiverse—anomic chaos in random agitation which, when plumbed with any of the old narrative myths by which we customarily attempted its measure (progress, say, or moral quality, or justice, or democracy), offered no certain or familiar soundings. In 1893 Adams was much less confident that a truthful history could be told. He knew that every fact spoke in a confusing gaggle of voices, none of which could claim privilege by merit of rank or longevity or provenance. What was needed was some scheme by which to organize the clamorous whole. What was needed, he understood from his Tahitian history and from his sensual apprenticeship to LaFarge, was an artist's ability to perceive and communicate essence. In a letter home the novice watercolorist had confessed, "I study in vain to find out how he does it, though I see all his processes." The accomplished historian marked the lesson: a work by LaFarge was "not an exact rendering of the actual things he paints, though often it is near enough to surprise me by its faithfulness; but whether exact or not, it always suggests the emotion of the moment." In *Mont-Saint-Michel and Chartres* he recounted the legend of Roland as it was understood at the time and not as it might have been corrected by scholarship, explaining his choice this way: "The poetry is history and the facts false."

The crisis of that Crisis Summer was the severest financial panic and recession that the country had ever known, a crisis surpassed only by the Great Depression of the 1930s. Henry's finances seem to have been secure, but those of his brothers Brooks, Charles, and John were threatened. Brooks tells the story in his editor's introduction to *The Degradation of the Democratic Dogma*, a collection of Henry's essays on history:

> Not knowing what else to do, I telegraphed to my brother Henry, who was spending the summer in Switzerland . . . to come to me at Quincy, as no one knew what might happen and I feared the worst. . . . Henry, like the good fellow and the good brother he was, answered my telegram and letter in person. . . . I had something else beside my pecuniary embarrassment to talk about. I had my incomplete manuscript and Henry in my house, and I had no mind to lose what was to me such an invaluable opportunity. So one day . . . I produced my potential book and said to Henry: "Please read this manuscript for me and tell me whether it is worth printing or whether it is quite mad."

The manuscript was Brooks's *Law of Civilization and Decay,* a work in which he meant to show that civilizations live, grow, and die according to inescapable laws of development. The financial panic lent a mood of urgency to his authorship; current events seemed to demonstrate his thesis. In his quest for scientific rigor Brooks followed the path trod by many another thinker seeking to establish a narrative, anecdotal field upon the quantifiable and precise ground of science, a path that the philosopher Stephen Pepper describes in his root metaphor theory: Brooks found a potent metaphor and systematically made it literal. In the *Law* he elaborates the language of thermodynamic science, seeing all civilizations as being endowed with a stock of energy and finding that the law of energy dissipation is as relevant to races and cultures as to steam engines.

According to Brooks's scheme, the ruling emotion of a civilization's early phase is fear. As a civilization matures, fear is displaced by greed. All the energetic virtues that were rooted in fear gradually decay, allowing less energetic virtues to emerge. Martial strength is displaced by economic and legal cunning; imagination, by calculation; emotion, by rationale; artistic expression, by scientific dissection. The rise of scientific and economic rationalism thus marks a decline in the culture's vitality, and the civilization will wither from a lack of energy unless and until it's infused "with new energetic material" through contact with a stimulating, fearsome, more primitive culture.

In support of this thesis Brooks marshaled the history of the world: detailed accounts of trade relations, of treasures hoarded and transported, of the distribution of witchcraft accusations in preindustrial European towns, all of which bore upon the relative advance of greed over fear, science over art, economic over religious values.

"If I live forever," Brooks wrote twenty-six years later, "I shall never forget that summer. Henry and I sat in the hot August evenings and talked endlessly of the panic and of our hopes and fears, and of my historical and economic theories, and so the season wore away amidst an excitement verging on revolution."

The excitement was mutual. Brooks's ideas found fertile ground in Henry. On the precise lawns of the family home in Quincy, under the large sycamores that still shade a corner of the yard, or in the garden, amid the roses and rhododendrons and bee balm, just south of the ivy-covered library where the portraits of two presidents hang, Henry began to grapple with theories of history, theories of historical change and development, theories that could, if they proved strong enough, impose shape and coherence on the unruly chimera of event. *Mont-Saint-Michel and Chartres,* begun nearly ten years later, and the *Education,* written hard on its heels, were the product of his effort to make sense of a world in which "all he could prove was change." Both owe their existence to Henry's encounter with Brooks's grand organizing scheme of history. The Crisis Summer was the beginning of Henry's effort to understand the forces that drive history, the forces that bring overall shape to the flow of minutiae and detail.

Here is Adams's own third-person explanation of the two works, from a chapter of the *Education* entitled "The Abyss of Ignorance," which covers a European visit in 1902:

> Any schoolboy could see that man as a force must be measured by motion, from a fixed point. Psychology helped here by suggesting a unit—the point of history when man held the highest idea of himself as a unit in a unified universe. Eight or ten years of study had led Adams to think he might use the century 1150–1250, expressed in Amiens Cathedral and the works of Thomas Aquinas, as the unit from which he might measure motion down to his own time, without assuming anything as true or untrue, except relation. . . . Setting himself to the task, he began a volume which he mentally knew as "Mont-Saint-Michel and Chartres: A Study of Thirteenth-Century Unity." From that point he proposed to fix a position for himself, which he could label: "The Education of Henry Adams: A Study of Twentieth-Century Multiplicity." With the help of these two points of relation, he hoped to project his lines forward and backward indefinitely, subject to correction from anyone who should know better.

"Thereupon," Adams concluded the chapter, "he sailed for home."

Some critics have praised Henry Adams for accurate prediction, as if this were the highest measure of his worth as a historian. As early as 1861 he wrote in a letter, "Some day science may have the existence of mankind in its power, and the human race commit suicide by blowing up the world"—a prediction he was fond of repeating, and evidence enough for some to think he foresaw the development of atomic weapons. In the years after 1893, as Adams elaborated a theory of historical change, casting it with conscious irony into the rigid form of scientific law, he offered other predictions. The history of thought, he said, displayed certain phases, corresponding to the phases of matter known to scientists. The five physical states— solid, liquid, vapor, electric, and ether—had their parallels in instinctual, religious, mechanical, electrical, and ethereal modes of thought. By rigorously applying a "Law of Squares" (which he invented for this purpose) to these phases in history, Adams found that a historical era lasted a period of years equal to the square root of the length, in years, of the previous era. Taking the mechanical phase to have begun in 1600 and to have lasted until 1900, Adams suggested that the religious mode of thought had lasted ninety thousand years (three hundred, squared) and foretold the decline of the "electrical" age in something like 1917 (seventeen and a half being about the square root of three hundred). The electrical phase would give way to the "ethereal" phase, which would last about four years and "bring Thought to the limits of its possibilities" in 1921.

"This prediction," says James Truslow Adams, a critic who wanted to validate Adams's science by an appeal to the pragmatic test, "has been fulfilled in a way that no scientist could have dreamed possible when Adams wrote. In 1925 came Heisenberg's new quantum theory and in 1927 his principle of indeterminacy. The law of cause and effect simply evaporated before a world of dumfounded scientists."

Well, perhaps. Or perhaps the existence of virtual institutions— virtual schools, virtual shopping centers, virtual workplaces— along with the success of postmodernist epistemologies that dismiss concern for "truth" as a quaint atavism are clearer signs that the etherealization of culture has brought thought to its limit. But I think the argument that Adams's theories are science is undercut by his too-obvious whimsy; there isn't much logic and there's even less science behind his invention of the Law of Squares. He doesn't even try to defend the artificially rigid scheme it imposes. All in all it seems to me that Adams's predictions have more in common with the biblical fulmination than the precise, scientific monograph.

While the phenomenon he points to—the increasing pace of cultural transformation—is real, the science is pure window dressing.

No, Adams employed his science ironically, in an effort to show that science itself was both the product and the harbinger of social decline; he might have said of science what he said of the newly discovered forms of radiation, that it seemed "positively parricidal" in its effect, for it undercut the culture that produced it just as X rays undercut the scientific theories of the day. What he owed to Brooks was not a scientific approach to history but a newfound sense that history could be rendered orderly in detail only after its overall flow had been described—and he and Brooks agreed that the flow was downward, toward decline and disintegration.

Adams cast that message into now this, now that metaphor: the history of human thought was a river, flowing down to a dead level sea, whence it would never rise again; it was a comet, rounding the sun with geometrically increasing speed, hurtling on into the void; or it was a dynamo, an inscrutable pure force, a thrumming machine made all the more frightening by the complete absence within it of any human or spiritual element.

That his science should speak through such a variety of metaphors is but one reason to suspect that what Adams was offering was not a scientific philosophy of history but something else. Another reason is found in his failure to provide any mechanism of historical development, any necessary process by which one era gives way to another. Certainly Adams had read the preeminent "scientific" historian of the nineteenth century, Karl Marx. Certainly this man for whom life from an early age was made of warring opposites would have noticed the role that dialectics plays in Marx's work, where it models just such a necessary process, and certainly Adams would have understood that dialectical materialism gives Marxist philosophy of history whatever claim it has to the title of science. But Adams, dialectical thinker if ever there was one, makes no such use of dialectics. Indeed, he fails even to mention it in this context. In creating a "science of history" based on his arbitrary formula, Adams most likely meant to satirize the idea that his chosen art could be transformed into science, and it's likely that a prime target of the satire is Marxism, whose Panglossian optimism he would have found particularly grating. (We know Adams was irritable with Marx. "This beats me," he penciled into the margin of his copy of *Capital.* "Nothing more German was ever written than this complication of value, values, and forms of value.")

Neither as a scientific historian nor as a sort of Brahmin Nostradamus ought Adams to impress us. He was after something else in his later theoretical writing. He perceived—he marked the passage in his Pascal—that "the empire founded on opinion and imagination reigns for a while and is sweet and unconstrained, but the empire of force reigns forever." In the years following the Crisis Summer of 1893 he began to survey this empire of force, to divine its laws and logic, its genesis and result. He could take nothing true but relation, for the universe has no fixed points or privileged observers, and where others saw progress he saw at best change and at worst decline. And he saw with great clarity the most important change of the late nineteenth century: "Modern politics is, at bottom, a struggle not of men but of forces," he wrote in the *Education.* "The men become every year more and more creatures of force, massed about central power-houses. The conflict is no longer between the men, but between the motors that drive the men, and the men tend to succumb to their own motive forces." Political volition (and with it, the excellences of character that all the Adamses had cultivated, indeed the very ground upon which politics as a moral vision could be lived) was disappearing from the world, yielding to the not-so-subtle, invidious encroachment of the dynamo, the ineluctable logic of commercial and economic development, the transformative logic of steam. Power was becoming more centralized: a score or two of men controlled the forces, the powerhouses (both literal and figurative) of the emerging industrial economy, and these men, like those who served the machines, were forces as dumb as their dynamos, men "who could tell nothing of political value [even] if one skinned them alive."

This, in Adams's view, was the culminating failure of education:

the world failed the knowing self by having become too confusing, too chaotic, too inhuman. The ignorant student might apprentice himself to kings or kaisers and still learn nothing, for no one knew anything anymore, and increasingly there was nothing to be known. Here was evidence of a law of civilization and decay presented as thermodynamic irony: the concentration of force results from and produces entropic decline of a culture.

At times Adams spoke of himself as a "Conservative Anarchist" or a "Conservative Christian Anarchist." Here, too, he demonstrated his capacity to understand the world, even himself, ironically. He allowed that the party ought properly to have a membership of two, since the party's great debt to Hegel, the principle of contradiction, required that any affirmative be immediately negated in order to establish its truth. "In some respects," says J. C. Levenson, one of his many biographers, the label was just "a term for his confusion," a term describing "someone who resists centralization but anticipates (often with morbid glee) his own defeat with a general cataclysm to follow." But when we look beneath the gentle self-mockery, we see (could any irony be richer?) that the patrician Adams, grandson of one president and great-grandson of another, was the first thinker of any stature to essay an anarchistic philosophy of history—if by that term we understand not simply a philosophy of history produced out of hostility to government, but a theory that attempts to understand the development of the empire of force in history, and which does so impartially, and which therefore of necessity—for the sake of clarity, of elegance—takes as given some assumptions that an anarchist could readily embrace. In *Mont-Saint-Michel and Chartres:* "Absolute liberty is absence of restraint; responsibility is restraint; therefore, the ideally free individual is responsible only to himself."

"One sees what one brings, and at that moment Gibbon brought the French Revolution," Adams wrote in the *Education,* explaining why *The Decline and Fall of the Roman Empire* emphasizes class antagonism and ignores religious monuments. What one brings is determined in part by what one needs, and what counts as necessary is shaped as much by historical circumstance as by any purely personal taste. And so every generation has brought a different Henry Adams to his work. The trajectory can be traced in the literature.

In 1929 Adams is a historian of "the first or almost first rank," a scientific historian albeit an amateur in science, and the only man (according to James Truslow Adams, writing in the *Yale Review*) to attempt "to subsume the multitudinous data of human history under a strictly scientific law."

In 1935 Adams is clearly a scientific historian: "He thought history should be a science," Roy Nichols reports in the *New England Quarterly*, "a science which should be absolute and which should fix with mathematical certainty the path which human society must follow."

In 1941, James Stone (in the *New England Quarterly*) finds in Adams a philosopher of history who understands that only through faith can we "close with the Mystery," and who nevertheless remains skeptical of all faiths, even those founded on science.

By 1947 Adams is "no scientist" but an "armchair, or philosophical scientist," one who is "dominated by the intellect and yet rebels against the tyranny of reason" and therefore ultimately repudiates science (Charles Glicksberg in *Scientific Monthly*).

In 1956 Adams wants science to step in and adjudicate the perennial debates of politics and philosophy, and in wanting this he is such a thorough anticipator of modern social science that "intentions and goals . . . concealed in modern social science may be illuminated by a retracing of his search." In 1956 Adams is also a relativist, aware of the arbitrary foundations of knowledge: "History remained [for Adams] 'a tangled skein that one may take up at any point, and break when one has unravelled enough. . . .' The historian, it turned out, was purely arbitrary. What end or purpose might be discerned in history, the historian had supplied it" (Henry Kariel, *American Political Science Review*).

In 1958 Adams is a moralist and a disappointed reformer, a man whose hereditary reverence for the Constitution was sorely tested

by nineteenth-century corruption (George Hochfield, in his introduction to *The Great Succession Winter and Other Essays by Henry
Adams*).

By 1964 he becomes both "the cool historian and the impas-
sioned poet," a technological determinist with a tragic, Manichean
vision; his fatalism makes him the sad melodramatist of history's irreducible clash between the Virgin and the Dynamo, between technology and a pastoral ideal (Leo Marx, *The Machine in the Garden*).

In 1976 Patrick Wolfe argues in *New England Quarterly* that
Adams's domestic affairs—his relationship to his wife and her suicide—are the key to understanding his pessimism and despair. One
year later, Adams is seen as the personification of Wallace Stevens's
"connoisseur of chaos," a man who knows that "a violent order is
disorder," that "a great disorder is an order," and that "These / Two
things are one" (Mutlu Konuk Blasing in *The Art of Life*).

By 1981 Adams had become an "antimodern modernist," a vital-
ist, a "twentieth-century Aquinas" whose work was "as precarious
in its dialectical unity and as dependent on faith, at bottom, as the
Thomist synthesis had been" (T. J. Jackson Lears in *No Place of
Grace*). Adams was also newly seen as the husband of the tragic
Clover, as the man who tried and failed to understand and protect
her, as the man whose Brahmin sensibilities were changed for the
better by his contact with her Transcendentalist leanings (Eugenia
Kaledin, *The Education of Mrs. Henry Adams*).

By the late 1980s Adams could illustrate the principle (which
has advanced upon us as the human population has grown) that no
one person can be treated in isolation, that individual biography is
properly seen as a product of the group. In Paul C. Nagel's *Descent
from Glory: Four Generations of the John Adams Family,* Henry is
"either the wisest or weakest of the Adamses," for he saw clearly the
family penchant for acting as if it had hope when it did not, and he
chose to exercise his pessimism on the sidelines of public life, running first to Europe and then to the twelfth century. In Patricia
O'Toole's book *The Five of Hearts: An Intimate Portrait of Henry
Adams and His Friends, 1880–1918,* Adams is but one member of a

group of friends (John and Clara Hay, Henry and Clover Adams, Clarence King) whose life stories intersect and intertwine and are profitably told together.

And in 1995, in my novel, *Panama,* Adams becomes a detective threading his more or less perceptive, necessarily idiosyncratic, completely fictional way through murder, scandal, and corruption in nineteenth-century Paris. I lighted on Adams as the central character for several reasons. I found him personally engaging; contradictory, provocative, witty, and dyspeptic, he fit no easy pattern, at least none I had been trained to see. Then, too, the author of the *Education*—a man "aching to absorb knowledge, and helpless to find it"—seemed a natural choice for a detective, that most epistemological of heroes. And Adams seems to me to have faced down a kind of pre-postmodernism: aware that the orienting traditions of political life were crumbling in the face of industrial and social change, aware too that in their absence the comparatively arbitrary ground of individual experience would by default become the measure of our knowledge (including our knowledge of right and wrong), Adams nevertheless found a manner and means of continuing. And this, it seemed to me, this perseverance in the pursuit of moral vision, has always been the defining purpose of the detective as a literary type and one great source of the genre's appeal.

In the coupling of paired opposites there is something essential to our humanity. Male and female, hot and cold, knowable and recondite, predictable and risky, orderly and chaotic, animal and spiritual, and all of the thousands and thousands of other pairs that sense and logic can discover: we inhabit always a median. Whether we do so by nature or through an act of volition is difficult to say. It is our habit as humans to abstract from our lives extremities of sense and conception which we then imagine mingling to shape our experience. The habit, the need, is elemental. Even the cadence of doubling, in speech, is reassuring.

So in a way Adams's anxiety at a future shaped by an unprecedented, unchecked, undoubled power may be taken as typically hu-

man. There are other aspects of Adams's life that can remind us of
our humanity, despite his erudition and Brahmin refinement, his
ironic distance, his persona of a provocative and dissembling po-
seur. There's the very human young man of the early letters, struggling to break from his family, alternately exhilarated by his freedom in Europe and mindful of the family's censure of frivolity.
There's the brother who grapples with an elder sibling's judgment
and rejects it to make his own path, a path more suited to his habitually ambivalent cast of mind. There is the widower, broken in
two by a suicide he anticipated but could do nothing to prevent,
and there is the shy old man, childless, devoted to the children of
his friends, who much preferred the company of women and children to that of the powerful men of his acquaintance. If this portrait
of Adams is fetching, it lacks the darker strokes that would make it
complete. After the Crisis Summer of 1893, Adams began to express
anti-Semitic sentiments in his correspondence, holding world Jewry
to account for finance capitalism. His distaste for mass society was
also a distaste for the masses, especially for the waves of immigrants
whose political presence diluted the influence of his own circle and
class. He can be seen as a curmudgeonly xenophobe, muttering
against a world that wouldn't abide by his will.

"Adams," says Levenson, "took a position just one step away from
desperation, and he sometimes lost his footing." And well he might:
he lived through the first fossil fuel revolution, the era of coal, and
saw that this transformation in the relationship between humans
and their world must transform politics and governance and everything else, and transform it continually. Often he must have felt
alone in valuing, or even in perceiving, what was being lost.

Adams knew that by the last decade of the nineteenth century
something new had been created. He knew that this new thing, the
industrial nation-state, would so alter the world as to make it un-
recognizable to someone born in the nineteenth century. He also
knew that the defining element of this new world was its command
of power. For a time he immersed himself in figures on coal, the
tonnages produced and consumed, thinking that the facts of the

black rock itself could symbolize the energies it released. But eventually he settled on the dynamo as the image that best represented the truth of the era: "He began to feel the forty-foot dynamo as a moral force, much as the early Christians felt the Cross," he wrote in the *Education,* describing his encounter with the hall of machines at the Chicago exhibition of 1900. "Before the end, one began to pray to it; inherited instinct taught the natural expression of man before silent and infinite force."

Adams saw that the imperatives of technological development would produce an evil that had no name, an evil whose outlines were just discernible in the secular worship of the industrial strength of the nation-state, and in a polity whose commercial development, ruled by the compulsory and apparently apolitical logic of industrial power, left little room for moral statecraft and even less for moral life. Adams saw, that is, the thing that the twentieth century would eventually have to name: fascism. His understanding of this uncompensated usurpation of politics, his suspicion that no balance with this force could ever be struck, and his resulting fear for the future—fear that drove him, *pace* his brother's theories, to undertake his culminating art—make him a compellingly contemporary thinker, a twentieth-century thinker.

We can appreciate Adams all the more as the Faustian costs of our scientific, industrial culture become increasingly obvious. His "scientific" philosophy of history, like a cruel and deftly managed portrait, reveals without caricature the limitations and weaknesses of its subject. That it was meant as a work of art, not science, he makes plain in one of his letters: As he told his confidante, Lizzie Cameron, in 1910, no one seemed to get the joke of his asking historians to submit to a science of history that would demonstrate conclusively the decline of a culture shaped by science. (He added that he had "so declawed the argument" that "it couldn't scratch," and that he didn't think he would get the joke himself if he weren't its author.) His artistry was exercised in pursuit of this truth: a world that knows no higher authority than the testimony of individual experience is a world plunged into chaos, a world in which each self is its own place of worship. This was the meaning behind his colossal presumption in drawing a line of development between Chartres and his own education: that transit described a profound loss. He wrote about himself not as an autobiographer but as an artist employing the forms of the historian he had been. As an artist in the multiplicitous present, his respect for truth led him to work only with material that he could know with certainty.

"Henry was never, I fear, quite frank with himself or others," Brooks Adams wrote, suggesting that we shouldn't believe Henry when he says that he learned nothing of use. But perhaps Brooks did not sufficiently appreciate the dialectician in his brother, or the Socratic irony by which Henry could honestly profess to know nothing useful to life in the world as it had become and yet still possess a certain practical wisdom. His wisdom, just visible in his life and work, consisted in this: the artistic enterprise is itself a metaphor for the human condition, and it can provide grounding to those who let themselves be taught. In the rules of form and process lies a higher authority, an authority that might yet salvage us from total subjectivism and the world it produces, a world plunged into the chaos of individuals colliding like atoms—"seventeen million times a second, like automobiles in Paris," Adams joked—a world that seems to clamor all too loudly for organization by the peremptory exercise of force. Often Adams seems to have felt too keenly the loss of cultural unity to accept any consolation, any attempt at metaphysical bootstrapping. Throughout the *Education* and his later essays on history he declines any solace whatsoever. But even so: he lived his life in responsibility to his muse, and in his work there are times when he seems to suggest that a modern foundation for intersubjectivity can be found in the processes of art.

Recall the plan that Adams set for a pair of volumes, one rooted in twelfth-century unity, the other in twentieth-century multiplicity. In that paragraph we see evidence of the artistry that lay behind not only *Education* and *Chartres* but also his ten-volume history and the two novels he published under pseudonyms. Adams presents himself in *Education* as an Everyman for the age, a seeker of wisdom in the new multiverse. In that chapter, "The Abyss of Ignorance," he lives on the brink of despair, in a kind of exile—exile because it is the nature of the human to know. In a world that has seen the old absolutes of religion crumble and the new authority of science assert itself on ground no more absolute than human convenience (by which even contradictory theories can both be true, if they serve), where do you find a footing? And what will save us from those whose resolution of this problem depends solely on power, on the nihilism of sheer assertion in the face of the void? This is what Henry Adams learned, and it contributes to the relevance that his work and thought have today: his search for pattern in history—his attempt to make sense of its broader movements, his attempt to craft, out of the materials of the historically given and with an artist's latitude and integrity, the threads of narrative which alone give meaning and context to the random gibberish of detail—this was the beginning of his journey home.

The Hand That Wounds

The San Gabriel Valley of California runs west to east, from Los Angeles to San Bernardino, on the southern flank of the San Gabriel Mountains. For a long time it was a center of the California citrus industry, and many of its small towns grew around railheads for the shipment of oranges. Twenty years ago in the rural parts of the valley the orange groves were still a presence. They rose north of Foothill Boulevard, rank upon rank, covering the wide alluvial outwash plain in orderly rows. Foothill Boulevard is old U.S. Route 66. It was immortalized on film and television as Hollywood's avenue into possibility: in the eponymous television show of the fifties, George Maharis and Martin Milner piloted their Corvette eastward on it toward adventure, and a decade before in *The Big Sleep* Bogart himself took Foothill east, out of the city and into the sparsely settled night, in a silvicultural version of the wilderness sojourn that mystics and detectives endure before returning, enlightened, to the city.

In the town of Claremont, about halfway between Los Angeles and San Bernardino, nobody packs oranges anymore and Foothill has long since been absorbed by civilization. It's a four-lane divided highway now, banked with shopping centers and developments and flooded with traffic, most of it local. For all but a block or two the time-and-temperature clocks and Bob's Big Boy Burger signs shoulder aside the rows of palm and eucalyptus that used to frame the view of the (frequently) snow-capped mountains, the view that made Foothill a scenic drive in the country. Occasionally the road breaks free to course through a vacant, unirrigated parcel ("Two acres! Will build to suit!"), but the lonely scrub there is no celebration of the antediluvian wilderness that once filled this valley. It's more of an inadvertent touchstone, a bulldozed, litter-filled baseline against which a true measure of our hubris can be made. The greater Los Angeles metropolitan area lies in a desert, and its importation of water is measured in millions of acre-feet per year.

When I arrived in Claremont in the summer of 1978 to attend graduate school, the first thing I noticed were the trees—not the eucalyptus and palm, which can be found in the surrounding towns, but the deciduous species whose anomalous canopy begins abruptly at the town line. The trees are an artifact of a town ordinance passed long ago that gives property owners a tax break for growing them. A broad-leaved tree is no small investment in a semi-arid region, but the good citizens of Claremont responded to this civic prompting by planting an amazing number of them. You can walk the wide back streets of the town (street numbers painted on the curbing, on-street parking prohibited overnight) sheltered under a roof of aspiring green. In autumn there are piles of oak and maple and poplar leaves gathered at the curb for pickup. If you yield to impulse and crunch through them, and can manage to ignore the flat, louver-bladed palm fronds, the stray cactus spine that has been swept up, and the ubiquitous piping underfoot that feeds the sprinkler systems and makes every yard seem, on anything more than a casual glance, less a natural occurrence than a studied construction with mysterious plumbing and hidden works, you just might believe yourself to be walking the streets of a Pennsylvania college town. Claremont is, in fact, used as a convenient and locally exotic setting by the movie and television crews who go there every few years from Hollywood, just over an hour to the west by freeway. The sprinklers don't show on the screen.

I went to graduate school to continue my studies in political philosophy, having that summer just completed a master's degree with a thesis on John Dewey. I held within myself an ambition I would scarcely admit: not just to study political philosophy, or even eventually to teach it, but to become a political philosopher, to make an original, revolutionary contribution to the history of political thought.

This was less grandiose than it may seem. Thomas Kuhn's *Structure of Scientific Revolutions* had suggested to me that revolutionary thinkers aren't born, aren't necessarily geniuses, but are largely made by circumstance. And I had read Sheldon Wolin's history of political philosophy, *Politics and Vision,* which treats political philosophies in a very Kuhnian way, as responses to periods of social and political crisis: Plato at the beginning of the end of the city-state, Machiavelli at the birth of the nation-state, Hobbes in the wake of the English Civil War, Marx in the crisis brought on by the Industrial Revolution. It seemed to me that a niche had been created for the political thinker who could comprehend the vast confusion of the ecological crisis and who could elaborate its consequences for political forms. I aspired to fill that niche, less out of egotism than a Hegelian notion of instrumentality. Hegel (whose work emerged from revolutionary chaos in Europe—*The Phenomenology of Mind* was completed within earshot of Napoleon's cannon booming at the battle of Jena) attempted to rationalize history, to find within it a breathtakingly immense logic. All of history is the necessary development of the Absolute Spirit, which struggles toward its own more complete manifestation in the world. The Absolute is opportunistic, even cunning, and works through us in ways that are beyond our ken or volition.

Hegel's is an essentially Christian vision. The birth of the Absolute in the world is the birth of human self-consciousness, the moment we ate of the fruit of the tree of knowledge, and history (or History—the biography of the Absolute) is the complex narrative of our redemption, the story of our eventual repatriation to Eden. Napoleon, Hegel thought, was doing History's work by forging the French people into a new, more compact social form, the imperial nation-state, a form necessary for the complete realization of social consciousness among us.

I too thought to serve History, as thinker rather than soldier, and in all humility was studying hard, the better to be its agent.

And so I went to California to get a Ph.D. I went with Frank, practicing hunter and political philosopher, who had been something of a mentor for me. We came straight from an eastern university where Frank had been a lecturer and I had been his teaching assistant. He had studied at Claremont years before and was still technically a student there, pending the completion of his dissertation, a broad-ranging critique of the antiecological foundations of modern totalitarianism. He wrote a recommendation that helped get me in, and when his contract was not renewed for the fall it seemed perfectly natural for him to join me.

Housing was expensive in Claremont. We soon decided we'd have to share the costs, and after searching for leads on a cheap apartment for several weeks among Frank's circle of friends we broke down and solicited the help of a realtor. Stan was a classic example of the type: white belt, white bucks, a dry and hearty handshake. No, he couldn't think of anything in our price range unless . . . maybe . . . he'd have to talk to this woman who sometimes rented out her garage. It was empty. The last time she rented it out it had gone badly. "It's not much. Housing here is tight. They really ought to be building, and believe me they will. I'd say in five years you won't see many orange trees in town." He said this not with regret but as a fact of life, as a circumstance of opportunity. Our problem, he made clear, was that we had come at a bad time. Our trouble was "a temporary blip in the market."

Political philosophers are a notoriously dyspeptic lot. Hume cursed the world that denied him fame, Machiavelli found his respite from an obstinate and unappreciative world in the peaceful sanctuary of his library, Henry Adams took pleasure in serving up dust and ashes to power, and Marx took out on capitalism an habitual crankiness aggravated by carbuncles. ("At any rate," he wrote to his collaborator, Engels, after a long day in the British Museum

Library, "I hope the bourgeoisie will remember my carbuncles all the rest of their lives.") The dyspepsia is properly understood as a symptom of exile. Political philosophers feel themselves homeless in the world, for they long to be citizens of the worlds they build in theory.

I was no exception. What had me living unhappily in the world was the enormous distance between our political and economic culture as it is and that culture as it would be if it were reconstructed on an ecologically sound, sustainable basis. Nowhere could that discrepancy be more obvious than in the greater metropolitan catastrophe of Los Angeles, a city built on the general acceptance of that enormous ecological mistake, the automobile, a city that languished in a fool's paradise of sun and warm breezes only because its desert environs were successfully disguised by the outright theft of water from other ecosystems. I flinched every time the sprinklers outside the library came on, drenching the quadrangle's golf-course lawn with water—not just because I was startled, but out of a sense of moral offense as well. The water had no business being within three hundred miles of the California desert.

Ecology is a moral vision, one in which the injunction to live a sustainable life implies an acceptance of limits. From the vantage of this ethos the San Gabriel Valley was an illusion worthy of Disney. From the perspective in time suggested by political philosophy (wherein all the thinkers of the past two thousand years are contemporaries, equally present, equally alive, their essential selves being not flesh and blood but words and ideas in the world) and ecology (which teaches us that the cycles of nature are often measured glacially, geologically), Los Angeles was a temporary blip on the planet, as unreal as any bit of stagecraft. As yet homeless in it, I held myself aloof from it, rather the way you might hold yourself back from a friendship with an unsavory character whose path briefly crosses your own. For me Foothill Boulevard was not an avenue of escape into some urbanite's confused image of an orderly, espaliered, orange-blossomed wilderness, but an avenue that stretched, both ways, into the heart of the modern insanity.

In my thesis I had argued that while John Dewey typified the turn-of-the-century progressive movement's concern for preserving democratic forms in an era of industrial capitalism, he had also provided an answer to a question that had not yet been asked. His work offered an appropriate foundation for an ecologically sustainable, democratic society. With my adviser's direction and encouragement I found in Dewey's *Art as Experience* a coherent system of thought that neither separated humans from nature nor offered any grounds for placing some humans in power over others. By challenging our faith in absolute truth, and by recognizing instead that what we call knowledge is the result of a process that unites the knowing animal with its environs in an essentially aesthetic experience, Dewey offered a sympathetic ground for developing the unity I had come to perceive between democratic forms of government and ecologically sound forms of culture. That unity was most obvious in Dewey's theory of knowledge—his epistemology—where he made clear that he was endeavoring to overcome the centuries-long tradition of various "spectator theories of knowledge."

A spectator theory of knowledge, Dewey said, proposes to explain how certain and knowable truth is discovered. It does so by abstracting the elements of subject and object, self and world, from the seamless whole that is the experience of inquiry. In doing so it creates a problem: a gulf between self and object, humans and nature, that can never be fully bridged.

Dewey didn't need a bridge because he refused to create that gulf. He saw the creation of knowledge as the definitive creative act. It came not as the result of a brief inspired moment but at the end of a process, a series of discrete states unfolding in time, a process in which knowledge is not discovered or uncovered but forged by the knower in his or her interaction with a problematic, sometimes obscure, sometimes cognizable environment. Media and purpose, world and mind, each interpenetrated the other. Instead of freezing inquiry into a snapshot and labeling the parts ("subject" here, "object" there), Dewey wanted us to analyze the movie, to see the temporal structure of the process of learning, and to use our knowledge of that as the ground upon which to lay the foundations of political relations. I judged him to have resolved the problem satisfactorily, and said as much, and titled my thesis "Toward an Ecological Epistemology: The Political Philosophy of John Dewey."

In historical survey courses of political theory, when Dewey is covered at all, he comes after Marx, for he was born before Marx died, and the two men had tackled the same order of problem— what to make of life in the modern industrial age. But from an ecological perspective, Marx offered brilliant systemic analysis without fully resolving the issues in front of him. You might even say that Marx was just another technocrat, sanguine about technology's ability to insulate us from nature and want, confident that the turmoil of politics would be displaced by rational, scientific management, optimistic in his belief that the forces of production, once they were brought under collective rather than private control, would be obedient servants, powerless to shape and control us. One of Marx's quarrels with capitalism was that private ownership of the means of production tended to dampen the enormous energies of development, as monopoly and the concentration of wealth into fewer and fewer hands blunted the spur of competition. Marx wanted to liberate those energies so that the exploitation of the earth could proceed more quickly.

History, Marx told us, was driven by the inherent tensions of human economic production (by class conflict, by the alienations of industrial production), not by the logic of some romanticized, self-generating Absolute Spirit. The necessary, inevitable resolution of these tensions would be the culmination of history. In this Marx had retained enough of the influence of Hegel to agree with the latter's dictum that "The hand that inflicts the wound is alone the hand that can heal it," while disagreeing about what that hand was. As Marx saw it, the various estrangements of modern life—the estrangement of self, from self and other and nature; of humans, from the product of their work; of knowing subject, from known object—would be gloriously transcended once the socialist revolution came.

Since I saw in that revolution the continued exploitation and domination of nature, I didn't think so.

Dewey, too, had been influenced by Hegel, but came to reject what he saw as the "artificial schematism" of Hegel's idea of history, which did Procrustean injustice to the facts and imputed to them a spurious necessity. While rejecting the artifice, Dewey retained Hegel's essentially aesthetic desire to overcome the "noxious dualisms" that beset philosophy and experience. So far from being a technocrat, Dewey had written poetry. (Much influenced by the example of Blake, I tended to romanticize artists and to think of poetry and dark, satanic mills as mortal antagonists.) His was bad poetry, which some janitor salvaged from the trash and from Dewey's own better judgment. But even so I counted it a sign of appropriate sensibility. Marx could never have attempted poetry!

There were, to be sure, a few retrograde elements in Dewey's work. For instance, there was the small matter of Dewey's obvious approval of Francis Bacon's famous characterization of science as a kind of Grand Inquisitor. "Experimentation," Dewey says in his paraphrase, "must force the apparent facts of nature into forms different to those in which they familiarly present themselves; and thus make them tell the truth about themselves, as torture may compel an unwilling witness to reveal what he has been concealing." No doubt Bacon reached for an apt analogy, but (as Wayne Booth has said) there is no innocent art. To someone studying classic texts for evidence of the intimate links between domination of nature and domination of humans, Bacon's words were almost too perfectly an example of what I sought. Dewey needed to be saved from his approval of them.

As it turned out, this wasn't difficult. In his epistemological defense of democratic forms, Dewey warns that our intellectual constructs are necessarily tentative. There are no absolute truths, no transhistorical certainties. There is only "warranted assertibility"— the temporary knowings that come to us from inquiry, which (if it is to be successful) must be free to criticize and to reconstruct the beliefs and dogmas and institutions we inherit and to discard what no longer carries us to the ends we seek. With the vantage of historical distance, I could see as Dewey hadn't that the attempt to dominate nature was no longer effective. I could see as he hadn't that we now had to make ecological sustainability the irreducible bedrock of our ethical systems. I could see more of History. I was willing to forgive Dewey for having been born before me.

Within a week Stan convinced his prospect to rent to us, and Frank and I moved into a barely converted two-car garage behind the home of Gattie Holmes, a retired piano teacher. Diminutive, tan, besneakered, white-haired, she had surprising, lively brown eyes and a teacher's smile, the half-suppressed smile of one who is continually charmed by the scamps of the world but thinks it best not to reveal this, lest the scamps take too much advantage. When the curtains in her living room were open we could see the matching grand pianos on which she still gave occasional lessons to kids. Stan had to overcome a great deal of resistance on her part, for the last time she had rented out the garage the tenant, a student, had had a nervous breakdown.

The garage was basically one big room, no kitchen, with a rug that covered most of the bare concrete floor. At least the garage doors had been replaced. In their stead was the garage's one redeeming feature, a set of built-in bookshelves that filled the entire wall. The craftsmanship was amazing. Finely filigreed and detailed, the shelves would have been more at home in some baronial mansion than in a cinder-block structure nearly devoid of windows. The boxes of books I had laboriously shipped to myself before hopping in the car with Frank didn't half fill them. "They *are* nice," Gattie said, running her hand along the smooth wood finish when I admired them. Her previous tenant had built them. "That's all he did, every day, for about half a year. He didn't pay any rent. He built these instead. Sand, sand, sand." She paused to pick her words carefully. "He was obsessed."

We did as much as we could to appear normal. Frank was a great fan of opera, as was Gattie, it turned out. I think she enjoyed raking leaves in her backyard to the distorted strains of *La Bohème* cranked through a cheap stereo played too loud. She was so taken by Frank that she could tolerate other, more disconcerting habits of his, even his preferred method of relaxation. There were no deer to scout in Claremont, so after long bouts with the typewriter, and especially in the days right after the meeting with his adviser in which he was told he ought to focus his dissertation, prune it down, and concentrate on one thinker—Hume, say—Frank would take his pistol (he had left his deer rifles in storage back east) and practice dry-firing at an imagined target across the yard. The point of this is to squeeze the trigger of an unloaded gun until the hammer clicks home, with no motion of the gun barrel. He would do this from a standing position in the garage, aiming out the open doorway, his face an expressionless mask of concentration. The first time Gattie raked her way into his line of fire and looked up, she almost fainted.

In the meantime I had enrolled for classes. The school had offered sizable salaries to lure a number of famous professors out of retirement back east. One of these was Herbert Schneider, "John Dewey's graduate student," I was told, who had studied with him at Columbia, succeeded to Dewey's chair in philosophy, taught for many years, and retired. Schneider then had a sort of reprise of his career for a decade at Claremont before retiring again, apparently for good. But now, I found at the registration desk, he wanted to teach one more course: "Classics of European Thought." It was likely to be his last appearance in the classroom.

The bookstore listed no required readings. At the first meeting the puzzle this created was not resolved. Schneider handed around a few photocopied pages from Plato's *Republic* and announced, simply, "Next week, Plato." He was obviously old, to the point of near infirmity, though he spoke clearly and his mind was sharp. When he held his arms out to reach for a paper or book, his body shook. His wrinkled neck rose loose from the crisp circle of his collar. The muscles had shrunk with age, retreating, leaving him a wardrobe fitted to a man who no longer was. Could he have meant to assign us just a few pages of reading? Or were we to focus on these in light of everything else Plato had written?

I assumed the latter. While I plowed into Plato, Frank grappled with David Hume. I would return from classes to our garage to find him sitting at his typewriter, pistol holstered on his hip, immersed in the *Treatise of Human Nature,* reading, typing, reading. To Frank, Hume soon came to stand for all that was wrongheaded in the western tradition. Hume began with a healthy skepticism about the foundations of our knowledge, but rather than accommodate this skepticism with political structures grounded in acceptance of diversity of belief, he searched until he found a bedrock value against which all else would be measured: custom, understood as the carrying forward of the project to dominate and control nature. If something served this end—which was, according to Hume, the objective long-range interest of the race—it was good. If it did not, or if it hindered that end, it was an encumbrance and a bad thing. Some races of people, of course, did not perceive their own long-range interest clearly. They neglected to develop and exploit nature as thoroughly and as effectively as white English-speaking peoples did. These laggards held back history, thus giving license to white Englishmen to expropriate them from their holdings. For dramatic effect, sometimes when Frank heard me approach the garage he would draw his pistol, point it at the book, and declaim, "I have you now, you corpulent Tory bastard!"

No two people who are not bound by the most intimate of ties should have to share quarters as close as a garage, even a two-car garage. Frank and I both made efforts to absent ourselves from our garage as much as possible. I took my studies to the library, where each week I would try to read as much as I could of Plato, or Augustine, or Aquinas, or Machiavelli before Schneider's seminar. I let my other studies slip. These were the classics, and ignorance of them was inexcusable. I would return to the garage just in time to fall exhausted into bed. As often as not Frank was gone. He made a habit of long, late-night walks.

His walks often took him past the house of Douglass Adair, a professor at one of the Claremont colleges who had killed himself more than a decade before. Frank had Adair's posthumously published collection of articles, *Fame and the Founding Fathers,* which he read thoroughly and repeatedly. There was a bond between the two of them, formed in part by dedication to the same subject matter (one of Adair's essays was about Hume's influence on James Madison, and it was crucial to Frank's effort to hold Hume responsible for the sad shape of the world around us) and in part by a more personal circumstance: Frank's graduate-school girlfriend had studied under Adair. The woman had gone on to become a novelist and had drawn on both of them in equal measure to create the central character in a university novel she had written and published some years before. That character, an exuberant, gun-wielding poet and opera buff, kills himself. I am sure that the weight of this connection bore on Frank as he walked the gently sloping sidewalk past Adair's house, looking for some clue to the circumstances that had animated his departed Doppelganger. What had his girlfriend meant to tell him by casting him in the same mold as a suicide?

I was no stranger to the night streets of Claremont myself. On the way back from the library I would wander, taking different routes, passing the quiet homes of people whose lives I knew nothing about, mulling over my reading while feeling a sharp loathing for the suburban sprawl around me. I kept a low kind of wariness, listening for a certain kind of click. Hidden in those trim California lawns were sprinkler heads that could rise of a sudden in the night, prompted by some mechanical timer, to spray dry lawns and bordering sidewalks in sibilant darkness, away from the jealous eye of the sun, with water spirited from the Colorado River. A careless walker could get wet.

The regular grid of avenues seemed a sorry denial of the constant flux of the outwash plain beneath them. That plain has a gentle slope—one foot in every twenty, interrupted here and there by the artificial level of a manicured collegiate sward or a private swimming pool surround—and is made from the same dry gravel that falls continually in the canyons a few miles above Foothill, where its steady whispering, quiet as mouse claws on wood, marks the San Gabriels as among the fastest eroding mountains of the world. The huge storm drains on the north-south streets had been called to my attention by a genial department chair: "Don't think it doesn't rain!" Winter storms off the Pacific cause the mud slides that affect the whole region, slides that descend and join to form stodgy, intermittent rivers, carrying the mountains downhill, toward the sea. The houses I walked past stood in the way of a force as irresistible as the flow of time, and yet knowledge of it was as effectively repressed as the evidence of the city's addiction to autos, which were swept from sight in the evenings, consigned to the grid of back alleys that bisected every block like a central gutter. In their way the mountains were like the philosophies I studied, great systems erected on bedrock certainties, decaying under the withering power of life in the world. It was folly to mistake either as permanent.

In Schneider's seminar there was an older student, a man in his thirties, who was known to all of us as Fat Jack. He was plump and peremptory and unpleasant. Academic passions are notorious for the narrowness of the objects to which they attach, but even by academic standards Fat Jack's preoccupations were finely focused. He was interested in Bentham's Deontology, and every chance he got, he raised the subject or asked a question about it. Deontology, the *Encyclopedia of Philosophy* informed me after the first class, is "the science of duty," at least etymologically. More broadly, it refers to theories of ethics that hold that some actions are obligatory without reference to consequence. ("The popular motto 'Let justice be done though the heavens fall' conveys the spirit that most often underlies deontological theories.") Jack's obnoxiousness wasn't found solely in his desire to steer the conversation or even in his cavalier use of polysyllabic words. These are the ordinary ways in which bids for academic dominance are made. What earned him the undying enmity of every member of that seminar was his tape recorder. He would arrive early and take a seat next to the chair at the head of the table and then defend that empty chair against all comers, so that Schneider would have nowhere else to sit but next to him. From his place at the great man's elbow, Jack recorded every word he said. This, alone, was not unforgivable. Fat Jack might have served posterity by recording Schneider's last course. What we found impossible was his habit of ostentatiously turning the machine off when any one of us spoke, so that his machine would record only Schneider's answers, never our questions.

At the second meeting we discussed Plato. Fat Jack began the meeting by asking, for the second time, his regular question about how the ideas under discussion related to Bentham's Deontology. Schneider managed some sort of answer before turning the question aside to take up his agenda. "Let us read," he said. And in a quavering voice, holding a magnifying glass that I recognized as coming from the compact edition of the *Oxford English Dictionary,* Schneider read to us from the mimeographed sheets he had given us. His hand shook and his voice paused on occasion when the words in front of him swam too far from his narrowing range of vision. At times he brought a hand up to cover one eye, perhaps needing to pin down a moving word with a sharpened, unifocal gaze. He pressed on, managing in spite of the wavering glass and the troubling eye to do justice to the meter and rhythm of the language. When he came to the end of the passage, he paused. Even Fat Jack was silent and respectful. "Plato is poetry," Schneider said, simply. Then, resting the magnifying glass on the table with a soft bump, he looked up at us, arrayed silently around the table. "This," he said, "is high art."

And so began a semester-long introduction to a different vision of political philosophy, one that showed philosophy to be something other and more than a response to social and political crisis or the work of an unknowable Absolute writing its inexorable story through us. There was a lesson here, waiting for me, and soon it became clearer.

One day I found the courage to speak to Schneider after class. How would he like, I asked, to read my thesis? It's about John Dewey. . . .

He agreed, and I dropped a copy off for him at the Graduate School offices with a note asking for an appointment after he had read it. I was surprised that he asked me to meet him at his house. Perhaps he didn't have an office on campus. Long before the appointed day I located the address. It was an old house, old for that area, meaning it appeared to have been built in the twenties. Made of dark wood, it had wide porches to provide shade from a sun that could no longer penetrate the canopy of deciduous trees. The front porch was screened, and through its silver and shadow I couldn't see anything. I made that street part of my regular route to the college, walking past it at least twice a day. From Dewey, through Schneider, to me: the path of historical continuity seemed as elegant, as breathtaking, as any of Pythagoras' theorems, any of Plato's dialogues.

When the time came, I climbed the porch steps and immediately faced one of those moments of displaced anxiety in which a minor uncertainty grows large enough to stymie. Should I knock here, at the screen door, or enter and knock on the front door proper? Where does the public space stop and the private space of the house begin? I mooted this back and forth, wanting above all to get it right, reading the house for clues. The front door was open. I'd knock on the screen door.

A voice within bid me to enter.

I did not immediately find Professor Schneider. He sat off to the left, in the room beyond the porch, a kind of study open to the kitchen and dining area, which I faced as I entered. His home felt like an old person's. Its furnishings all dated from an earlier time, not in some studied and fussy reconstruction of a period but in that gentle and settled way that bespoke continued use and satiety, a kind of peace. You could see that the occupant had long since stopped buying things, that his habits had been formed and his needs accommodated long ago. The cookware in the kitchen was white enamel. The toaster was a two-slice model similar to the one my grandmother kept in her room, with a vaguely art deco design and a fuzzy braided cord. The house had a familiar smell of once-damp plaster and of simple food recently cooked. When I came through the doorway, I found Schneider in a chair to my left, sitting at an old wooden desk with a few scattered papers and books upon it. Very little of the afternoon sun was penetrating the window behind him. The house was cool and pleasant. He smiled at me. "Come in, come in. Please sit." He gestured toward a plain wooden folding chair near the desk.

I know that in the conversation that followed Schneider told me of Dewey's farm in Vermont and of how he and other students would gather with him there. He told me of the interest Dewey had developed, late in life, in conservation and the problematic relationship between culture and nature. I know that we talked, for a time, about the seminar, and about the work I was doing for it. But I really didn't hear much beyond the first words he spoke to me after I sat. "John," he said, patting the cover of my thesis softly with his white, deeply lined hands, "John would have liked this."

It had never occurred to me as I wrote my thesis that I might someday meet someone capable of rendering such a judgment, someone who could casually refer to Dewey as "John" and interpolate his tastes in a way that bore directly on me. When I'd sat at my desk in my parents' attic through the long Delaware summer, reading, sweat dropping off my nose and dimpling the page, Dewey had been a name and some ideas in a dozen books, no more, as dry and as distant from me as an encyclopedia entry. I felt a peculiar sensation, like but unlike those looping epiphanies that send you reeling because you're suddenly disconnected from some certainty upon which you've built your life. It was like the lurching moment you get stepping off one of those moving sidewalks you see in airports. I was dizzied by connection, by being suddenly rooted, dizzied by having the inchoate flow of time cohere into solid, humanly scaled form right there, in the dappled light of Schneider's study.

Of course, I was flattered. I carried the satisfaction of that meeting like a prize back into the sunshine and through the rest of my week, where I coasted through all the ordinarily troublesome encounters of graduate student life, enduring both seminar bullies and autocratic professors on the strength of Schneider's words.

But eventually I couldn't help thinking: John Dewey. Not a set of ideas, not just an historical niche in the onward flow of thought, but a flesh-and-blood human with a farm and friends, likes and dislikes, quirks and comrades. He was a person with whom, had the world worked out only slightly differently, I might have talked. I saw that until that moment I'd treated political philosophy as a sanitary cargo of abstraction, safely manipulable words on a page, words whose intersection with the world lay in the past (and, maybe, in my future: perhaps, someday, someone would read what I had to say and find their lives changed by it). There, then and there, I was forced to begin to think of it differently.

In thinking about it I came to see that in my way I was not all that different from Fat Jack. He, too, was struggling to find his footing and had simply chosen a different ground in his effort to escape the Heraclitean flux. An absolute of ecological sustainability, an absolute of a single moral truth: what did the difference matter, if certainty were to blind you to possibility, to alternatives? We all want to believe that what we ground our lives on has more substance and permanence than the shifting ground of individual will, that there's more to it than our own (or another's) say-so or convenience, and yet fealty to any absolute is a certain path toward decay and irrelevance at best, injustice and extinction at worst.

In Schneider's seminar I came to understand more completely what I had only begun to spy in Dewey's work. The logic of form, of conscious human activity in the pursuit of meaning (which is to say, of art), is a middle ground. Art is distinctly of us, a product of our consciousness and will, and is as common and as various as we are. And yet art is also beyond us, not simply a product of our will, but shaped by all sorts of forces impinging upon it: social context, historical context, physical constraint. Art is not, as the romantic cult of the artist encourages us to think, about self-expression.

("Self-expression?" I was to hear an art teacher colleague say, para-phrasing Virginia Woolf. "That's therapy. Don't send me students who want to express themselves.") The process by which art is made and known has a discoverable structure. If artifice is the hand that wounds, perhaps in the logic of artifice we may yet find the hand that heals.

Once when I came home from an afternoon of classes I found Frank and Gattie in our garage, sorting through some things in a cardboard box. Long ago Gattie had written a series of radio dramas on the lives of the great composers and now she was showing Frank the scripts. In the warm afternoon sun she told us how both ra-dio and she had been young, how to her and her friends anything seemed possible, possible even that radio would nourish love of good music to the far corners of the earth. She had a collection of small ivory busts in the box, too, and she took these out to show us. "Ah, Puccini," Frank said, taking it up in his hand. "He's my favorite."

"I know," she said. And she gave it to him.

Frank made progress on his dissertation. "Read this," he said to me one day, thrusting Adair's book at me, open to the title essay. I read it. In it Adair describes how college-educated men of the founding generation attended schools that were in the thrall of the Scottish Enlightenment. Hutcheson and Hume would have been part of the curriculum. And in the theory of moral sentiments ad-vanced by Hutcheson was a telling metaphor. He addressed himself to the problem of morality, noticing that there was no single cate-gory of actions that were, everywhere and at all times, good and no other category of actions that were always bad. All depended on context. How then to judge the good action from the bad? Judg-ment, Hutcheson decided, could be accomplished only by disinter-ested third parties, whose inner moral sentiment would cause them to attach feelings of praiseworthiness to good actions and of blame to bad. This theory was elaborated with metaphors and analogies drawn from the stage. We are all actors, performing in front of an audience that serves as the disinterested observer and judge of our

moral character. But what of action—such as the founding of a republic—for which there was no ready audience unaffected by consequences yet fully cognizant of the delicate intricacies of context?
Who would judge then?

The philosophers of the Scottish Enlightenment answered with a
single voice: history. Only future generations would be disinterested
enough and knowledgeable enough to judge such actions fairly.
Those statesmen and thinkers whose actions and ideas were worthy of praise would receive it, in the form of fame, at the hands of
posterity. Those whose works were negligible would be neglected.
"Maybe," Frank told me, "Adair killed himself because he was worried he wouldn't become famous."

When I lived in Claremont, the orange groves north of Foothill
were just beginning to fall to development. Now I hear they are
gone. I hear that when you look at the valley from the mountain
heights, the tracts of suburban housing are a mosaic of red-tile roofs
and concrete spread on the valley floor, covering it like linoleum
unrolled and trimmed to fit the flatness. The change is bemoaned
by many, even by those of us who have no illusions that the orange
groves were anything like the wild, natural state of the valley, even
those of us who know that a restoration of the valley to its pristine,
pre-city condition would be an immense act of stagecraft. It has
been difficult for me to abandon the idea that in nature we can discover all we need to know about ethics. But nature does not exist as
an absolute outside of history. Our perceptions of it have always
been culture-bound, so the "nature" that is imported into political
thought is and always has been a human construct. There's a logic
to the history that brought us where we are, and it is a logic that
must be changed. What may yet ground us in our efforts is the
knowledge of our need and a critical appraisal of the forms taken
by our efforts to satisfy that need.

That, it seems, is work enough for history.

In Search of Virgin Forest

ver time I have tried to learn, as Aldo Leopold asked us, to read a landscape for its history. I am by no means an expert, but I have learned enough to make myself unhappy.

I began with that undergraduate course in geology, where I learned that some landforms are natural and some artificial. Having in the same place learned of the damage that humans do to nature, and being then an unreconstructed romantic, I much preferred the natural. As I learned how to read a landscape, I found pleasure in less and less of the outdoors. Ecology breeds misanthropy. What I wanted out of doors was to experience capital-N-nature, nature pristine, untrammeled, unshaped by human hands. I wanted to be away from the incessant presence of others of my own species. I wanted to participate, like Muir, in wildness as the hope of the world. Like Thoreau of the Walden idyll (before his hike in the distant, far-from-Concord wilderness of Mount Katahdin, where the forest struck him as "savage and dreary," "even more grim and wild" than he had anticipated, and where he felt not solitude but loneliness), I wanted to spend time in solitary contemplation, in communion with pure otherness and whatever it suggested, wanted to measure myself against some touchstone not of human making.

Everywhere around me I found evidence of the passage of others, evidence of their walks and works: paths, gum wrappers, stone walls, contrails, or once, typically but for some reason memorably, the roar of truck traffic on the interstate that crowds the Potomac River at Harpers Ferry, which drifted up to where I lay awake in a tent just off the Appalachian Trail. The machine in the garden, Leo Marx called it, suggesting with this construction that our own tools have replaced the serpent of Christian iconography.

In the woods of Virginia, above Harpers Ferry, I first noticed the bulbs that barbed wire makes in tree boles when it is swallowed by the wood, and which remain long after the wire is gone.

"In virgin forest, the ground is uneven, dimpled with pits and adjacent mounds," John McPhee tells us in an uncredited Talk of the Town piece in the *New Yorker* of July 6, 1987. In virgin forest, trees are taken down by the wind, levering up great root balls of forest soil. Gradually the trees rot away. "When no other trace remains of the tree, you can see by the pit and the mound the direction in which the tree fell, and guess its approximate size." This is not, it turns out, sufficient information to enable me to identify a virgin forest. Nor is the knowledge that a virgin forest is a forest that has never been cut. As my daughter informed me when I tried to explain to her what it was I had been looking for, "Every forest has trees that have never been cut." She was right. I had to sharpen the definition, and soon came to explain it the way the forester does, with language that smacks of euphemism: "Virgin forest is forest that has never experienced cutting activity since the time of European settlement."

Virgin status depends on what can be called the land's "disturbance history," a history that is not always clear, even to experts, from the records left on site. The surest evidence that a candidate piece of forest is virgin is documentary: an unbroken chain of legal title, say, held by owners who can truthfully say that the land has never been logged, and who are supported in this by the testimony of community folklore, by town records and histories, and by a conspicuous absence, on site and off, of evidence to the contrary. Many foresters won't credit a stand as virgin without supporting documentation. This is odd but appropriate—odd, given that for many people virgin forest symbolizes the antithesis of our culture and its bureaucracies of paper; appropriate, given that the concept of forest virginity is not a natural but a cultural category, a template we lay upon the arboreal ecosystem, an idea that we import to nature. To call a forest "virgin" credits it with having its own natural, nonhuman "disturbance history," and so takes note of the forest for having maintained its otherness, its continuity outside the most obvious graspings of human culture. But (Hegel again) what is is defined by what is not, and all things are shaped by complementing their opposites. By elevating to the status of distinguishing criterion our failure to disturb, we draw the virgin forest firmly into our history, for we use our history as the base against which its exception is measured.

In the summer of 1991 I spent a few hours one hot afternoon looking for the telltale pits and mounds of virgin forest on the northern flank of a hill in central Vermont, a hill not very far from one climbed by local Millerites on a late October evening in 1844 to await the rapture at the end of the world. I searched with a friend whose visit to Vermont was the occasion of this, my effort to give particular form to a long-standing (and, to that point, entirely too theoretical) appreciation of virgin forest. Besides a vague sense of appropriate terrain and the knowledge that the large trees a virgin wood in this region was likely to contain were sugar maples and beech, what we had to guide us were the reassurance I received from a consulting forester I knew ("You'll know it when you see it") and a woefully inadequate map put out by the Vermont State Department of Parks and Recreation. The map showed hiking trails in and around a state forest, some distance away. But there, separate from the other holdings, off by itself and outlined in bold ink, was a small tract labeled "Nature Study Area." I inferred that this was it.

I am no uncritical fan of inference. I would have welcomed knowledgeable corroboration—had sought it, in fact, only to have the college student staffing the information kiosk at the park entrance confess ignorance and advise me to return, later, when the ranger would be around. Because I had typically left matters to the last moment—my friend's visit would be over in the morning, and we had only an hour or two before dinner—that wouldn't work. We studied the map. No trails led to the nature study area, but it was clearly just uphill from a disused class 4 road. A thumbnail comparison with map legend said a mile along the road and half a mile up the hill. What could be easier?

We drove the abandoned road for a mile, parked the car, and looked for a likely trail. At first we walked up a woods road, a remnant right-of-way from some past logging operation. Any bushwhacking cross-country skier is familiar with these. Their purpose is extractive, not connective, and so they function a bit like the fake fish scales that are embossed on the bottom of waxless skis: travel in one direction is easy, travel in the other is frustrated. When you happen on a logging trail on a downhill jaunt you've suddenly got clear skiing. Find one on the uphill, though, and you face a multitude of choices as the logging road branches and branches again and again, each branch soon petering out into a vague cul-de-sac that is part clearing, part ordinary forest thinned by logging, which may or may not have been thinned enough to let you thread your way through, or (just as often) the trail dead-ends abruptly in an impenetrable, ski-snagging pile of brush—the tops that timbermen leave behind, which a firewood cutter would have turned into thick batons of stovewood.

Uphill was the right direction, given the map and what I knew of the provenance of virgin forests. I was guessing that our small ink-lined patch was somewhere on the unexploitably steep pitch we could see about half a mile ahead of us.

As we hiked we talked, and for a time we talked about Bill McKibben's book *The End of Nature*. McKibben explores the provocative idea that nature is over—that as an entity distinct from culture it has ceased to exist. In addition to the impressive sum of particular disturbances we've committed (extinctions, habitat transformations, genetic manipulations), it seems clear that we humans have affected the climate. Now, when you feel a warm breeze on your face in the spring, you won't know whether it's "natural" or whether it's a result of global warming. The possibility that it could be the latter is enough to establish that nature is no longer conceptually distinct from culture. We are, McKibben concludes, at a historically unprecedented dead end.

The topic was appropriately apocalyptic. The Millerites had climbed that nearby hill prepared to meet their God, and I was pretty much doing the same.

My companion didn't think much of McKibben's book. I had a hard time following his criticism, concerned as I was with orienting us and worrying about not finding the forest. And peripatetic though philosophy may be, it is difficult to hike up a steep hill and to think carefully at the same time.

Whatever else it is, virgin forest is not a natural tribute to the virtues of egalitarian democracy. The existence of virgin forest today is often the result of a historical concentration of property, of large tracts being held by single families for generations. Sale of land stimulates the exploitation of land: the payment of market price drives an owner to use land for market uses. In periods of population decline in Vermont, when land prices were depressed, loggers could take out a mortgage on a tract and pay it off in a few years with the lumber they cut. In periods of economic decline, when cash to pay property taxes was scarce, some on-the-margin landowners finally solicited logging operations in that woodlot they'd been saving. Virgin forest often survived undisturbed as a small percentage of undemocratically expansive holdings. One of the largest stands of virgin timber in the northeast, the 4813-acre Big Reed Pond tract in Maine bought some years ago by the Nature Conservancy, had 150 years of ownership by the Pingerees, a paper-milling family. Their total holdings in Maine amounted to something like 900,000 acres, a Long Island–sized forest of potential pulp.

Virgin stands like Big Reed Pond are exceedingly rare, especially in the northeast, especially in New England. They are unknown in Vermont. Hard figures are hard to come by; the consensus answer to the question "how much virgin forest is there in Vermont?" (a consensus of those I polled: a group that includes private foresters; county foresters; arboreal economists; the former director of the Vermont Wilderness Association; the current director of the Natural Heritage Program of the Vermont Department of Forests, Parks, and Recreation; various state park rangers and rangers-in-training; state forest public information officers; Audubon, Nature Conservancy, and Vermont Natural Resources Council officers; and a silviculturalist or two) is "not much." (Chris Fichtel, the director of the Natural Heritage Program, was willing to hazard some imprecise figures: old growth forest in Vermont might total a thousand acres, and of that probably less than two hundred is virgin.)

Vermont is now 15 percent clear and 85 percent wooded, a ratio that exactly reverses the ratio of the 1890s, by which time the search for lumber, the high price of wool, and the need for fuel and heat had combined to denude its hills. George Perkins Marsh, a native of Woodstock, Vermont, lived through the era of clear-cutting, and his comparison of the resulting floods to the milder spring freshets he remembered from his youth led him to investigate the role that trees play in retaining rainfall. He generalized from there. The resulting work, *Man and Nature; or, Physical Geography as Modified by Human Action,* published in 1848, is the ur-text of the environmental movement. Not coincidentally, it is also the first book to treat nature not as unchanging essence but as mutable entity. A history of my adopted town of Calais written eighty years ago reports that one clause of its charter required the settlers to reserve uncut "all pine timber suitable for a navy"—a stipulation that amused the author, Calais being a good 120 miles from the sea

and (at the time of chartering, before any settlement, in 1781) completely devoid of roads. But Calais is bisected by the Kingsbury
Branch of the Winooski, one of the five major Vermont rivers that
drain into Lake Champlain, birthplace of the U.S. Navy. Trees felled
near enough the river might be sawn to plank length and skidded
to a springtime "waterhead," whence they could be floated to a
mill—if not the fifty or so miles to Burlington, which was to become for a time the largest inland lumber port in the country. And
if the tallest trees couldn't negotiate the Winooski uncut, not even
on the annual flood, prudence would still suggest that some be as-
signed to the navy and left in place until roads could be had to
haul them. The British experience had demonstrated the wisdom of
naval timber reserves. By 1781 good masts were getting hard to
come by.

Eighty-five percent clear, 15 percent forested: that 15 percent
must have been worked exceedingly hard for lumber and fuel. By
the 1890s firewood had become scarce enough in Vermont that it
was imported from Quebec. The Montpelier and Wells River Rail-
road is said to have turned 100,000 cords of wood into ashes and
steam one mid-nineteenth-century year. Controlled, systematic experiments I did some years ago suggest that a good-sized clap-
board farmhouse with plaster and lathing on the inside, a four-inch
pocket of uninsulated, mobile air in the walls, and a pair of cast-
iron stoves (one parlor, one cookstove) might consume upwards of
fifteen cords of wood per winter in an unsuccessful effort to keep
the frost line somewhere behind the plaster.

As petroleum calories began to replace hardwood calories in the
chimneys and flues of New England, the demand for forest products
remained robust. Growth in paper use more than compensated for
the loss. All of New England was being cut. Bangor, Maine, became
the busiest lumber port in the world. Most of the virgin stands that
survived into the twentieth century survived by accident or over-
sight or because sawing them down would have been impractical,
uneconomical, or legally chancey: the slope too steep for lumber-

ing, ownership of the land contested in court, the wood too puny
to matter. (The phrase "virgin forest" conjures images of deep,
cathedrally canopied woods, but a good part of Vermont's virgin
forest is waist-high: it consists of subalpine scrub pine, trees that
grow gnarly and uncommercial on the slopes of Vermont's tallest
mountains.)

"Old growth" is not, as I once thought, a de-sexed synonym for
"virgin." A virgin forest is by definition an old growth forest, but
not all old growth forests are virginal. Old growth forests share a
variety of characteristics, and which ones ought to be considered
definitive is still open to debate, despite having been from 1989 to
1992 the subject of a series of conferences held around the country
by the U.S. Forest Service's National Old Growth Task Group. In an
old growth forest you'll find tip-ups (trees uprooted by the wind);
snaps (the dead stumps of trees broken by the wind); multiple canopy layers; deadfalls of various ages rotting on the ground, with
natural holes in the canopy above them; a diversity of ages of trees,
with the dominant tree in the canopy having attained a minimum
age of 150 years and also at least half of the average maximum age
for the tree. (Hemlock, for instance, lives to an average of six or
seven hundred years. An old growth hemlock stand would have to
be 300 to 350 years old, old enough to qualify it, in these parts, as
possibly virgin. In a process that isn't exactly consistent with one's
idea of "virgin," the tree's age is determined by core samplings.) An
old growth forest can have trees cut within it and remain an old
growth forest. Cut a tree in virgin forest, though, and the forest
around immediately falls, losing in that instant its purity, becoming
just another old growth forest.

How much virgin forest is compromised by the intentional felling
of a single tree within it? How many old-growth trees antedating
white settlement does it take to constitute a virgin forest? The U.S.
Forest Service has yet to produce standards for this sort of question.
That the issues involved in answering these questions have a more-
than-theoretical importance was borne in upon me as we walked

uphill. At one point we rounded a corner in the woods road and came, unexpectedly, upon a cabin shuttered up tight. Fifty yards from it stood a magnificent sugar maple, tall beyond reckoning, nearly four feet in diameter at the base, bent and twisted at the top of its bole but carrying this deformity with strength and substance. Obviously a tree of some age and distinction. Obviously a tree that a woodlot manager would have cut as a sapling to get it out of the way; that twisted bole was a pure waste of board feet. Did it have companions? Was this the edge of the virgin forest? Had we walked half a mile?

We explored the area around the cabin, evaluating each tree, both of us performing our versions of the complex calculations that the attempt to identify a virgin forest encourages. I thought: the one certain feature that a virgin forest can't have is sawn stumps. Are there any? No? How about other markers? (The stumps could have rotted into soil years ago, so their absence isn't definitive.) How old are the trees? Any particular tree in a virgin forest could be young and thin, an upstart raised in the gap created by a tip-up, but on the whole the dominant species should be tall, majestic, old. There should be a dominant species. Is there? Is that tree young and thin? Too young and thin? How many really obviously old trees are there here? What percentage? (Should I count?) How tall ought they to be, if this is truly virgin forest? Has drought or soil infertility or some other thing kept these trees from fattening? Suppose they're old but thin? Core samples would fix this with certainty. There's another good-sized tree. How far is it from the marker tree, the big sugar maple? Could this be virgin forest, this ground between them? Is the ground hummocky enough? Are those hummocks natural or artificial? Is that a barbed-wire bulb in the bole of that tree? Is that a hummock, or a big stone covered with moss?

The fluidity of the simultaneous and comparative calculations this required kept my eyes and thoughts moving, looking, judging, and I felt wide awake, called to this purpose. The not knowing, though, was frustrating. Too bad the owner of the cabin isn't around, I thought. (It was just as well, I learned later. Resident own-

ers on that hill—and there are a few, despite the lack of roads, the
area having been colonized by summer people willing to hike in—
can be unfriendly. Tired of surprise arboreal tourists in what is, to
them, a private woodland retreat, they tend to view the virgin forest
as an attractive nuisance, and they've been known to berate "tree
huggers" asking directions or, perversely, to steer them wrong.)

After a few minutes of investigation we decided that the rest of
the forest didn't measure up to the sugar maple. The trees were definitely younger, thinner, and not as tall; and so we had not yet found
the virgin forest.

We pressed on, continuing uphill. In time we came to a woods
road that passed laterally across the face of the hill, very near to the
base of the steeper part. This pitch, steeper than stairs and extending beyond sight up and to the left and right, looked promising. We
crossed the road and made our way through a dense thicket of small
saplings to get to it. The ground on the hillside was hummocky all
right, hummocky with outcroppings of stone, grey granites and
white quartzites held in the clammy fists of exposed tree roots.
There were no obvious saw-stumps. The trees, mostly softwood
with a scattering of beech, were substantial—smaller than the sugar
maple we had seen, but then maybe these species didn't grow as tall
as sugar maples. (Embarrassingly, I had forgotten to ask my consulting forester what species we'd find in the virgin forest, so we
weren't completely sure what sort of trees we were looking for.)
Was this it? We had absolutely no way of being certain.

It was almost time to return home for dinner. We limped laterally
across the face of the hill for a while, one-foot-up and one-foot-
down, trolling for virgin forest, thinking that if we were in fact
within it we might best discover this through contrast, through direct juxtaposition with the not-virgin forest beyond its border. This,
too, was inconclusive. Ultimately we concluded that we couldn't
know, not with what we knew, not with the information we had. I
felt the disappointment of having failed as host and guide. As we
turned to go, picking our way gingerly down the hillside, I volun-

teered to continue the investigation. I'd find out for us if we had been in virgin wood.

The sexual metaphor behind the term *virgin forest* is obvious. There's a racial element in its technical definition as well. The determining factor of forest virginity is the absence of "cutting activity" by whites, by Europeans, or (in a looser definition) by anyone, even natives, after the advent of Europeans. What is being said by this? Either the virginal status of the woods was immune to the exploitative depredations of Native Americans (and so the woods remained virginal, even after being clear-cut by stone axes, which seems to have happened here and there), or Native Americans are presumed not really to "count" as exploiters. The latter course is that taken by those who make environmental heroes of Native Americans, those who see Native Americans as having lived in a pure clear state of ecological grace. It is also the course taken by nineteenth-century racists, who denied pre-European indigenous culture full status as human civilization and who thought: Native Americans are just savages, so what they did was not done by human agency.

Why not drop the racial proviso and call a forest virgin if it has hosted no "cutting activity" whatsoever? Practically, there are difficulties: if virgin forest is forest that is documentably undisturbed, then the category can have little meaning for cultures that are nondocumentarian. Our land histories don't stretch back before white influx, and so without some racial criterion in the definition there would be no virgin forest at all. But that won't do. There are forests that are usefully distinguished for being old and unharvested. The term *virgin forest* has use and meaning in the world.

And even if we decide that documentation is not essential to the concept, "virgin forest" is European in genesis and application, a product of a worldview that tends to sentimentalize in one context what it brutalizes in another. To read the concept backwards into this continent's history—to root the term in pre-Columbian Native

American experience by failing to add the words "by Europeans" to its definition—does injustice by forcing the experience of non-Europeans into the constraining forms of the European worldview and its categories.

To a citizen of today's civil society, "virgin forest" is forest that is definitively wild. It is forest far from human culture, forest ready and available to enchant. We do find our own species less than enchanting, don't we? A virgin forest is a cul-de-sac in our culture's headlong rush to progress, a dead and peaceful end, an overlooked backwater that, in the transvaluation of nineteenth-century industrial values by twentieth-century experience, has become a cool clear pool of relief. The demand for such relief outstrips the supply. (In his article John McPhee was careful to shield the location of the Rutgers University–administered patch of virgin forest he visited, lest his readership create a sympathetic-yet-destructive increase in forest traffic. I have tried to do the same.)

We make of virgin forest a sacred space, taking it to be nature pure and essential. Maybe we find a hint of our culture's Puritanical heritage in this equation: spirituality flourishes only in the vacuum of sexual innocence. Like sexual innocence the sanctity of virgin forest isn't just current and isn't simply a matter of appearance or behavior. It reaches deeper, into quality of being over time, and so must be confirmed by history, by an absence in that history of a certain sort of experience. That innocence is absolute and delicate. One lapse and it's gone forever, even if all physical trace of the lapse is erased. The absence of sawn stumps is no guarantee of a forest's virginity. The violation could have occurred long ago. What it looks and feels like *now* is not necessarily what it *is*.

To accept this—to make an absolute and historical innocence of any sort a precondition to exemplary, transcendent worth—dooms all of us to a profane and uninspired life, for we are, none of us, that completely innocent.

As my friend and I walked down the hill, I turned the conversation back to McKibben's book. I wanted to pin down his exception to it. This is what he said: "McKibben has a naive and typically

Euro-American view of the continent as virgin wilderness that is now suddenly different. There's no sense that people have been radically altering their environment for millennia. The 'end of nature' thing has been said before—Heisenberg, I think, said something very similar after Alamagordo, that now we knew sin in a way we had never known it before, that here was an end to innocence, to nature. The end of nature seems to be a mood that people get into periodically."

"I have never knowingly been in virgin forest." I could truthfully say that when my friend and I started off, and I could truthfully say that when we climbed down. I can't say that now.

I went back to my consulting forester and mentioned to him, delicately, my difficulty in finding the virgin forest. "Oh, yes, of course," he said. "It's really hard to tell. You could walk through a corner of it and never know." Consulting foresters help tree farmers and other landowners with forest management, and state-certified consulting foresters must approve the management plans that qualify landholders for large property tax exemptions in Vermont. I got the impression, talking to this consulting forester, that virgin forests are to consulting forestry something of a professional irrelevance. People expect such a forester to know something about such a forest, and so to maintain the expertise necessary to professional success the forester will learn something about the subject. But the knowledge is casual and distant, taken like an inoculation against the improbable chance of a visit to some exotic place.

I returned to that area in the spring, in the company of a naturalist who had been to the virgin forest before. He confirmed my suspicion that the tourist maps keep the location vague in order to discourage casual traffic. After some indecision about where to leave the old road, we struck off over ground familiar to me. We walked for a time, stopping here and there to spy woodpeckers. Where my friend and I had crossed the lateral woods road and begun to climb higher my escort led me off to the right. The woods road ended in a thicket of saplings and grasping raspberry suckers.

We parted them as best we could and climbed over an unnatural pile of dirt that had served, before the saplings grew, as a sort of bumper preventing vehicular traffic.

It turns out the virgin forest is almost level. It turns out there is a fallacy involved in deducing from general statements ("Much virgin forest stands on slopes too steep for logging") to particular cases ("This virgin forest will be on that steep slope"). Fittingly enough, it's called the ecological fallacy. I would call my friend and let him know: we had been within stovewood-pitching distance. The ground in the forest was indeed pitted and humped, though not as much as I expected. There were snaps and tip-ups in great evidence. I counted twelve in close proximity, lying in different directions and in different stages of decay: they had fallen at different times, not in the same storm. (After humans, wind is the strongest force a tree stands up to, and from it they protect each other. The loss of one tree makes others more vulnerable.) There was even one spectacularly charred lightning strike. I felt majesty in the height and girth of the oldest of the trees, yes, and in the idea that these living things had been here, growing in the sun, long before the first European slogged his pioneering way up the valley below, reckoning potential pastures. But I was also aware that this knowledge was, in this woods, exotic: I had brought it with me. It had no necessary claim to be here.

The dominant species were sugar maple and beech, with an occasional hophornbeam (also known as ironwood) and spruce. We had timed our visit to be post-snow but pre-blackfly-infestation, and so the canopy had not filled out. The light on the forest floor was cool and full. I could imagine the dense shade the trees would make in the summer, a shade broken here and there by a warm splash of berry bushes growing up into the sun on the moss-softened skeleton of a toppled spruce. It was beautiful now; it would, I thought, be beautiful then.

As we walked I asked my fill of questions, each of which elicited additional information that I was too unwoodsed to have asked for: secondary succession in this area is mostly poplar and gray birch, the forest has been in uninterrupted evolution on this hillside since glaciation 12,000 years ago, snaps are like apartment houses for birds, blowdowns indicate thin soil. He could talk about the history of individual trees. This forest had been the subject of careful observation and inquiry.

At one point my attention was drawn to the ground and I saw there the rusted lid ring and the dull, rust-perforated shank of some sort of can, not a beer can but a food can. A bit of machine in the garden. Like a good Boy Scout ("Take nothing but pictures; leave nothing but footprints"), I pried it up from the soil and packed it away for transport out, not noticing the irony until much, much later: I violated my ethic in order to enforce it on someone else.

Virgin forest is not untrammeled forest. It's not a forest innocent of human passage. It's just forest that has never had "cutting activity." Finding a bit of industrial garbage there saddened me, but it might have saddened me more if I had not already had my ideas about the purity of the forest adjusted by one of the first things the naturalist had shown me. Nailed into each of the tallest and strongest trees, as part of an ongoing and otherwise unobtrusive study, there was an octagonal brass numberplate identifying the individual tree. The most certain way to know you are in virgin forest on that hill is to look for the glint of brass.

Zeno's Mall

C*'mon, c'mon, move!* I'm stuck behind a slow, droopy-jeaned, flannel-shirted man licking an ice cream cone. He's got a lumberjack's build—thin legs, stocky chest, and arms so muscular that the one that holds the cone can't rest at his side while he licks but must stick out, triangular, a meaty wing blocking traffic. *Let's go!*

I can't wheel around him. On one side there's a trash can backed by aisle-narrowing booths from a home decorator show, the kind of dismal trade show that mall managers are always getting up, and on the other side the prospect is crowded by an approaching rank of teenaged girls, a half-dozen of them in easy linear solidarity, giggling, watching for teenaged boys. I'm in the mall on an errand, a quick duck-in on the way home from the airport. My fellow shoppers are, frankly, a nuisance—too languid, too casual, too oblivious to movement around them.

This is a pet peeve of mine, this disregard, and I'm ready to shout, "Pay attention! Mind your part in the flow!"

It isn't just malls that bring this out in me. On city streets I get irritated by drivers who don't respect the idea—who seem incapable of *conceiving* the idea—that traffic is a stream extending behind as well as in front of them. To my mind a driver who stops in a traveled lane to discharge a passenger violates an article of trust, one I know is disproportionately important to my sense of a functioning social contract. Streets are dedicated to movement, no one has the right to block them for mere personal convenience, and this understanding is such a basic part of the deal we all accept by joining civic, automotive society that as far as I'm concerned your failure to honor it raises serious doubts about whether your capacity for other-regard is sufficient for social living.

This rudeness gets to me because I believe that a sense of history is a moral obligation, and I suspect that the inability to see traffic as a flow extending forward and backward has its origin in the same selfish, narrow-minded presentism that infects our politics and our social life. The driver who will inch along a public way, automotively loitering while deciding where to go, is a driver who lives too much in their own narrow, vehicular present, a driver who doesn't see connections forward and backward, a driver ignorant of obligation, one who believes that what is behind is safely passed and so doesn't bear thinking about.

At the mall, I'm after a baseball hat my daughter covets—my "Honey, I'm home" present to her. I'm on the lookout, nose up, as if I could detect sporting goods by smell alone, trying to peer over the clog of people that slows me down. I get around the big cone licker only to be stymied again by a glacial family of four, comprising an infant asleep in a stroller, a woman pushing the stroller, a boy of about six, and a shamble-limbed man. The woman has a leaning-back, shuffling gate and the man, unencumbered by a handlebar, walks like an R. Crumb poster, flashing sole with every step, his walk so sloppy, such an inefficient movement of mass through space, that you can be certain it never had the test of difficult practice, of long hikes teaching economy of movement as a virtue; the boy, bursting to run, seems reined in by some unseen parental threat or bargain. And it comes to me as I walk behind them eager to get by that what I am seeing in their inability to sense my haste is a form of physically induced trance. A yoga. Shopper's gait, that languid pumping, a sort of meditation.

Suddenly I understand, and relax.

Three antecedent moments lay behind my mall-walking epiphany.

One: the morning of the day before I had been sitting in a folding chair by a window on the conference-roomed second floor of a hotel in New Orleans, drinking coffee and listening to a panel of professors expound on Faulkner and Melville and Kundera. As I listened, the sun topped the low building to the south and shone clear and strong on my March-in-Vermont-cold skin, warming my face, and for a moment I gave myself up to it, the first strong sun I'd felt that spring: warmth, natural warmth, a simple delight. I listened but also let my mind wander and in that wandering surprised myself. I realized that I was actually glad to have gone to graduate school in Southern California.

I hadn't felt that way at the time. Besides thinking of Southern California as an ecological disaster area that I wanted to hold myself aloof from, I found the climate not the pure and inviting pleasure that had lured so many people out there but a pushy, intermittent taker of hostages. There were frequent smog alerts, days we were told to stay inside and to avoid exercise, anything that might make us breathe more deeply. So why did I recall it fondly?

What it was, I realized, was the sun.

Winter in Vermont is enough to make anyone remember strong sun fondly. But there was more to it than that. Sitting in that conference room I realized that while in Southern California I'd formed a deep and until that moment entirely subconscious association between political philosophy and the feel of sunshine on my body. The two had paired to form a kind of subliminal Platonism. Out of the cave and into the light of the Good: justice and light, philosophical abstractions and the sort of warm, buzzing, timeless afternoons that I hadn't known since childhood had become inseparably linked. All I needed was strong sun of a certain angle on my face and a ripe phrase or two—"Rousseau's stag hunt" or "the social contract," one or another of which the Kundera-speaker had conveniently provided—and the whole nexus of association came flooding back to me.

And so in that conference room in New Orleans I was led to recall the younger man I had been, a youth innocent of the difficult economy of attention we find we must manage with age, for then, as a student, I had known myself to have time for every worthwhile thing in life, and once again knew that the most worthwhile thing was to grapple with large, passionately apprehended abstractions in the good broad light of day. And yet I still knew myself, my older self, and knew that no matter what happened in the grappling, no matter what these panelists said about Faulkner and Melville and Kundera, I could be sure I wasn't about to overhaul my life on account of it. I was no longer staking my soul on the outcome of my learning, the way the me-who-was-a-graduate-student had been able to. Platonic warmth or not, I was no longer a thinker with all my being. Or, more precisely, my being was now too my history: the momentum of my life's choices had accumulated an inertia, a force too strong to be bent easily by a few lines of text or speech.

And there, hearing Kundera paraphrased (or quoted—I had lost the thread)—"And what is love but a kind of ceaseless interrogation? From which it follows, no one loves us as do the police"—I recalled those long spring Saturdays of my childhood, when my brother and I could pack a lunch into the fields and marshes along the Chesapeake and Delaware Canal and lose ourselves in them, lose all time-consciousness in the heat and the fragrance of tidal muck and the sunbaked smells of fresh straw and methane-rich manure. To the child I had been, every moment was a forest you could not see through, a marsh with no further shore, a great untrammeled space inviting exploration. In my childhood (it now seemed to me), afternoons made of these infinite moments had stretched out as an unfathomable freedom before me. Then, there, in that place, that's when I had known most clearly that I had time for every good thing.

This nostalgia stung me like an actionable offense. Why are adult days so short? How had this youth been taken from me? Who had taken it? I wanted names, wanted to talk to a lawyer, felt for a moment (typically American, this) that I must have standing to sue.

And I knew: innocence is a wicked indulgence when willed or worn too late in life. Better to let the memory of it taunt us.

Later that morning, moment number two: in the windowless cavern of the hotel ballroom I browsed the conference book fair and its rows and rows of booths filled with books from the year's academic lists. I had a research project in mind. At each booth displaying an introductory economics text I stopped, flipped the book to the index, and looked for two entries: "Georgescu-Roegen, Nicholas" and "entropy."

Georgescu-Roegen is a Romanian-born economist, recently retired from Vanderbilt University in Nashville, whose name might reasonably be found in the indices of introductory economics texts because of a book he published in 1971 with Harvard University Press. *The Entropy Law and the Economic Process* rigorously develops the idea that economic activity cannot and does not violate the laws of thermodynamics. This idea, commonsensical though it may be, has been enough to mark him as a maverick among economists. His work has generally been dismissed or ignored within the profession, notwithstanding the fact that Paul Samuelson (he of the million-selling introductory text) blurbed the book by averring, "His ideas will interest economists when today's skyscrapers have crumbled into dust."

The first law of thermodynamics, you may recall, holds that matter and energy can neither be created nor destroyed, only transformed. The second law, the law of entropy, says that even though the energy of the universe is a constant, the amount available to us to do work continually declines. The steel and iron and plastic and glass that move through our economy can be recycled, but the fuels that run industrial processes cannot. If there were no entropy process, if the energy content of fuel didn't dissipate with use (into heat, into motion of the air, into movement of mass against inertia), if it could be recycled, if an engine could be made that, running backwards, converted heat and motion into gasoline, we would experience no scarcity, no fundamental "economic problem," no outstripping of (presumably) infinite wants by (demonstrably) finite means of satisfying them. Without entropy we'd have a flow of goods too cheap to meter. Every useful thing that ever existed would still exist, fresh and new, and we'd have little need of economics, the science that studies the allocation of scarce resources among competing ends. Georgescu-Roegen's contribution to the march of economic science, then, was to show that it's physics—the science of thermodynamics—that makes economists useful.

It's a shame they haven't returned the favor. You won't find Georgescu-Roegen's ideas about thermodynamics in any introductory text. Samuelson blurbed but didn't include. One text does mention his earlier contributions to econometrics, the mathematical side of the discipline, and another has a nonsequiturish photo, unsupported by textual mention, whose caption acknowledges him as "one of the earliest environmental economists," but about entropy the texts are silent.

Their silence is a mark of mainstream economists' nineteenth-century-ish "no deposit, no return" attitude toward nature, an attitude that might be quaint if it didn't have enormous consequences for life in the world. Marxist or capitalist, it doesn't matter. Economists of all ideological persuasions specifically assume that economic activity has no cumulative effect on the environment in which it takes place.

You can see this clearly in a standard diagram found in almost all the introductory texts. In it the economy is modeled as two circular and opposing flows, money in one direction and goods and services in the other. In David Colander's *Economics* (Irwin, 1993—the text that has Georgescu-Roegen's photograph in it), money leaves households at nine o'clock for markets at noon and flows thence to businesses at three o'clock. Businesses take this income to the factor market at six o'clock, where they spend it as rent, profit, and wages, paying it all out to people who live in households, starting the cycle over. In the other direction flows an equal and opposite stream of goods and services: households provide factors of production (labor, natural resources, capital, managerial skill) to businesses, which transform them into goods and services for sale to people who live in households.

To be sure, Colander's model isn't a closed system—there are arrows darting into and out of the exemplary household (which looks a little like a monopoly hotel) and the exemplary business (a boxy, modern building with a pair of clean, cylindrical smokestacks). But these arrows don't indicate interchange between the economy and its environment. Those factory stacks don't spew smoke, and the house hasn't even got a chimney. The arrows are labeled "international connection." American firms and households trade with other countries; each is a point of tangency between our rootless "no deposit, no return" circle and the unrooted circles of other countries' economies. Never is there a sign that so much as a candy wrapper falls out of the economy to affect the environment, nor is there a hint that so much as a single barrel of oil comes from anywhere but a household. (Presumably the household supplying the oil is home to a shareholder in Exxon, who just happens to have barrels of the stuff lying about the living room.)

If your model tells you, even as a first approximation, that oil comes from households and not from nature, or that garbage doesn't go to dumps but is somehow fully taken care of by entrepreneurs who live in households, it's easy to fool yourself into believing that "pollution is simply a resource out of place" (one of the standard economic dogmas, logically entailed by the definition of everything as a potential resource) and that the absolute historical rarity of the industrial fossil fuel age is instead something approaching the permanent condition of humanity. (Colander's model isn't even a first approximation; it includes foreign trade, a second-order wrinkle.) If your model tells you, as a first approximation, that economic activity is in its essence an endlessly repeatable cycle, you'll relegate your discussion of pollution to the back of the book (as Colander does—Georgescu-Roegen's picture appears on page 641) rather than understand pollution—the production of valueless waste—to be an inevitable, thermodynamically entailed consequence of economic activity. Only if you believe in perpetual, entropyless motion can you believe in this economics as fluid mechanics, in this Newtonian economics of reciprocal and reversible flows, divorced from any grounding in nature, in history.

I was still thinking of these matters when I took my place at the next panel I attended, on Adam Smith, author of that eighteenth-century classic, *The Wealth of Nations,* the paradigm-setting text of market capitalism. In the discussion that followed the presentations and comments, one of the panelists allowed (moment number three) that Smith had aimed to make of economics "an ahistorical science of dynamics." Yes: economics as a science looks at changes in time but ignores history, the compendium of all changes in time. The wages-to-prices-to-wages cycle turns over and over, and the factor-inputs-to-commodities-to-factor-inputs circle turns over and over the other way, but the motor that drives these tandem machines, the irreversible engine that runs one way in time, is out of frame, offstage, unseen.

And I began to think: this explains why Georgescu-Roegen's ideas haven't achieved wider appeal. One function of the commodification of our world is the escape from history. The escape is no accidental consequence but part of what we are intending to buy. To spy the thermodynamic origin of wealth, to accept that time's arrow points at us, puts us too much in the world. It too clearly contradicts the dogmas of infinite creation and infinite self-creation upon which modern capitalism depends.

The next day, as I searched for sporting goods and found myself stuck in that flow of casual perambulators, I saw a connection between the shopper's meditative gait and the profusion of commodities around us. On one side bins of jellybeans in subtle pastels, on the other tables full of sweaters bright as jellybeans; between them exercise equipment clanks away in a booth mocked up as a living room, and every fifty feet an aproned teen prods the fringes of traffic, hawking some factory's thirty-five flavors of fudge. Rack after rack, shelf after shelf, bin after bin, too much to see, and in seeing that, I saw that the mall functions as a kind of church. Impatience is out of place, for the ordinary temporality of the world is there suspended.

Like a church, the mall is an awkward container for public life, a house unsuited to the body politic. It's hard to imagine soapboxes and stump speakers in its corridors. And yet it isn't typically private space, either. We gather there on Sundays and holy days, and like most churches a mall wouldn't serve well as a home, wouldn't sustain the physical needs of life. In its ritual, democratic promenade we achieve communal awareness while having a kind of respite from politics and the other disquieting features of the world outside its doors. The mall draws us with the solace of community, of equality, of shared purpose and vision and practice. We all want to be attractive, comfortable, smart, thin, young, pretty, leisured, entertained, distracted, consoled, serviced, served.

The community of consumption is more illusory than real and sustaining the illusion is costly, but we seem grateful for it. The dogmas implicit in the design and purpose of the mall offer a kind of self-transcendence, not just because in the mall we hope to accomplish a commercially promised transformation of the self but because there we encounter a kind of infinity. As Henry Adams knew, standing before a thrumming dynamo at the Chicago Exhibition in 1900 (feeling its force as a moral force, feeling that atavistic urge to pray), the encounter with infinity has always been among the strongest intimations of our spiritual selves that any of us are likely to know.

There are two kinds of mathematical infinity. One is the infinity of large numbers: for every number you can name, there exists a number larger. This is the kind of infinity we used to find in nature. It's what we seek when we want an experience of the unbounded: that childhood afternoon stretching on forever, a forest you can't see through, a continent with immeasurable reaches, a great blank white spot on one's mental map. We tend to confuse freedom with possibility and by habit associate both with nature, a nature that, to the American mind, was necessarily the objective correlative of our new-world brand of democracy. But we've grown up, populated our continent, cut down and seen through our forests, worked in the blank spots on our maps. We no longer have this kind of infinity. Nature has been brought fully into history and now is bounded by it. Wilderness survives only in managed pockets and nature itself has a history, the history of our transformation of it.

The second infinity is the infinity of endless division, the infinity that's the basis of one of Zeno's paradoxes. Imagine a tortoise, he said, crawling halfway toward its object, then halfway again, then halfway again, forever. It will never arrive at its goal. What is present and real to us is the infinity of Zeno's paradox, the bounded infinity of infinite divisibility. This, I realized behind that shuffling, glacial family, explains the popularity of the mall.

The mall is walled against nature, time, death, weather, change— against history and these, the many faces of its disappointments. The hurrier is the one who is out of place there. We go to the mall to celebrate our contact with that which gives us life and defines us—not the spirit, timeless and placid though that may be, but another ahistorical, placid infinity: commodities, the clothing and housewares and foods and trinkets and decorations and accessories and appliances with which we, through our discriminating selection of them, demonstrate our taste, the secret or public truths of our being, the qualities to which we privately aspire, the qualities we wish to announce that we have achieved. Individual commodities come into being and pass away—the law of entropy isn't violated—but we can, in the mall, experience something like continual renewal: like the hunting and gathering tribes that conceived of time as a cyclical rather than linear movement, we find in the passage of the planet's scarce material through our hands not the sorrow of a one-way flow but reassuring contact with an ever-freshening source.

Rack after rack, shelf after shelf, store after store, the objects available to us seem infinite. We try on new selves with each imagined purchase, exercising something of the spirit within by deciding what we want, who we are, who we hope to be. Even the sexual quality of mall walking, the slow, hips-forward, repetitive pumping of the peripatetic shopper: isn't spiritual awakening essentially an erotic experience?

And throughout the ritual of shopping, subtending it like a knowledge beyond need for speech, there is the experience of the infinite, a comfortable infinity of things to look at and try on. It's an infinity to lose one's self in. It's an infinity comfortably larger than whatever crowd we collectively can throw at it, even on shopping's busiest days; like the body and blood of Christ, like the sublime and infinite stretch of eternal grace, the mall's infinite supply of commodities is never noticeably depleted by our partaking of it. The mall reassures by telling us we do not signify. The sins our economy commits against the planet and against this planet's other peoples we commit collectively and corporately, and at the mall we see our absolution. Individually, separately, we are exculpated by reason of inconsequence.

The mall has become our opaque copse, our sacred grove, the recondite-because-unencompassable other we require to measure ourselves against, to humble ourselves before. No one could possibly fondle or size or even simply look at every available item. Like the fractions between any two whole numbers, the space of the mall is bounded but the items contained within it are in practice infinite.

Facing this infinity, one relaxes. There's not enough time to see everything, so why try?

Facing this infinity, one must slow down. There are too many possibilities to be had.

Facing this infinity, one begins to yield. Maybe, just maybe, life could be timeless once again.

Timeless once again! Oh, innocent shoppers, relax, relax. In the mall, of course you can relax. Suddenly, in the mall, away from history, there's time.

Parge and Strike

My pond emptied in minutes. Water shooting out the raceway carried off the pond's entire complement of ten-inch-long trout and all the crayfish that hadn't managed to burrow into the mud and hang on. Standing on top of the dam, next to the planking I had just pried out of the dam's bottom gate, I surveyed what had been revealed: a shallow valley, banks shiny with fragrant mud, about thirty feet across and a dozen feet deep at its deepest. Along the sinuous line where the two muddy banks converged ran Titus Brook, already scouring down to bedrock and clean gravel, held now by one less catchment on its way to the Winooski.

I was due downstream myself for a softball game in Montpelier, part of an end-of-summer tournament for the bar league team I play on. By rights I should have thrown my glove and spikes in the car and been on my way instead of watching all that water. But floods have irresistible appeal. Something in sinuous, laminar flow, in the control and release of channeled otherness, engages me. And not just me: the road commissioner says that when he grades the roads in mud season he always sees evidence of quite a few volunteer helpers, citizens who get out their shovels and scratch sluices into the dirt, encouraging the puddled snowmelt to drain from the roadway. Freud has an explanation but I think it too single-minded.

The metaphoric allure of participatory hydraulics isn't just genital. There's the attraction of pure experiment, of taking demonstrably effective action in the world, of seeing cause and effect immediately displayed.

The dam I had just opened is a hundred and fifty years old and is made of stone laid up in clay. It's a "thunderstorm" dam, according to Erlene (a native of the town, blunt, prodigiously competent, a local historian). If you size up the two penstock remnants that jut through its bottom—metal tubes about two-and-a-half feet in diameter, sealed at the upstream end—you can begin to decipher the term. The penstocks are larger than the stream flow. When they were open, powering the mill, the pond would have gradually drained. "They'd work for an hour, then close the penstocks and sweep up while the pond filled," Erlene told me. "But when it rained, watch out! They'd work like mad." In time their rainstorm work must have become more frantic. In time the forests that held back the runoff were cut.

The mill that helped turn those forests into beams and planks and clapboards, the mill that used this dam as part of its foundation, is gone. The stonework it left is beautiful. Rivulets trickle and spurt through it, sustaining lush moss, wildflowers, grass, making of the dam a hanging water garden. In the center of the dam the main cascade slides off a wide, stone-slabbed spillway, becoming for a moment a smooth green curtain before fraying and then exploding, white, into surf on the rocks below.

The waterfall is constant motion, shine, rumble. The stream moves through it and is gone.

The dam goes with the house, an old Greek Revival cape (tall white pillars on the two-story porch) just across the dirt road. The mill chase goes under a stone-arch culvert and along the foundation of the attached barn, gurgling against it continually in its downhill slide. Relentless, unheeding, regular: the flow of time itself. A few days before I pulled the plug (two-inch-thick tongue-and-groove planking, definitely oak, heavy with water), Kathryn and I signed papers promising to buy the house. We're to take possession on

Labor Day, two weeks away, the last day of summer, the last day of softball season.

The dam is one reason we're going to move four miles, down from our old hilltop farmhouse and into this small village. When we began carrying boxes of books into the barn earlier that summer, getting a jump on work that would have to be done before our semesters started, we'd cool off afterwards with a dip in the pond. I'd drift, carried by the current, toward the dam. No danger of being swept over—the escaping water is only inches deep. I loved to look down the spillway. It's a strange sensation, immersed in water up to your eyes, to look down, past a horizon of water, at a house. Some atavistic mammalian brain-circuit is profoundly troubled by the sight, and the unease is intriguing.

But then, early August, before we moved in, the water in the spillway slowed to a trickle and stopped, done in by heat and the long calendar cycle between summer and melting snow. More water was leaking through the dam than was being supplied by the brook. In a few days the height of the pond was halved, turning a self-cleaning swimming hole ("like a pool but no maintenance," we'd said) into a brackish sump held by a dam that sieved whatever floated down: leaves, branches, a thin algae scum.

I'd have to parge and strike it.

I found out later that two centuries ago, when settlers came to the area to exploit the power of its water, they'd have parged a dam like this with clay. (To parge is to spread a thin, maybe quarter-inch-thick layer of sealant, usually mortar, on masonry or stone.) A hundred and fifty years ago, I learned, they used a mixture of coal ash (fine particles, like clay) and sawdust (to give it body)—a mix too problematically toxic to think of using today. A hundred years ago, with the advent of the dynamo, the fate of the area was set, though it took another half century to play out. By the 1940s, when the Rural Electrification Administration got to my town, the local mill industries had long since closed down, moved to Montpelier and Northfield where they could be served by the regular power of The Grid. In the vestigial water-power villages of Washington County you can find moss-covered dams, some still holding back their mill pond, others fallen into disuse, tall stone walls that bridge shallow, tree-filled valleys.

To strike is to run mortar into the joints of a masonry wall, filling and finishing the joint. As I chipped out the old, loose mortar with the chisel-pointed back of my brick hammer, getting ready to strike in the new, it became obvious why no one makes fieldstone dams anymore: between every two stones is a joint, a potential leak. I worked from a jump board, a plank thrown across saw horses whose legs I placed into five-gallon buckets to keep them from disappearing into the muck. Sometimes beneath the old mortar I'd find soft, gray clay.

For a week I repaired the dam by day and played softball at night, standing in right field while my team worked its way through the playoffs. I've played for the same team ever since arriving in Vermont seventeen years ago. I, the only historian among us, can't remember from season to season how we've done, whom we've played, what our opponents' names are.

I don't play to remember. I play for those few moments of transcendent coordination when I lose my mind and simply act, as though by instinct; when my body surprises me with its skill, its competence.

(The surprises come less often than they used to. I'm getting older. We're all getting older. We play teams whose median age undercuts ours by ten, maybe fifteen years.)

By day, behind my dam, standing above the muck on my jump board, I'm a neighborhood attraction without quite being a neighbor. People stop by the pond-hole's grassy, weedy lip to offer what they know of the history of the dam or to ask me questions. Sometimes, to do the joints near the top, I cling precariously to the corbeled surface in front of me, doing a little nontechnical climbing with a thirty-pound bucket of mortar and a fistful of tools: trowel, striking iron, pointing trowel, slicker. Each one works best on a different kind of gap. I try to memorize faces, try to sort locals (whom I'll see again, once I move in) from passers-by.

Behind the dam it's hot, down out of the breeze, and while the mud drying in the sun makes it plenty humid, there's no pond to cool off in. The striking iron and the slicker are too slow. With them I can apply only small bits of mortar, over and over, filling basket-sized holes a kernel at a time. With the pointing trowel I can slice a good-sized gob of mortar out of my bucket, flip it at the wall, then press it deep into place and smooth its surface in one quick, efficient motion.

The work is mechanical and it frees my mind to wander. Perhaps because I've spent some time with realtors lately I find myself thinking of Pierre Joseph Proudhon, the early-nineteenth-century French author of a revolutionary pamphlet that asked, famously, "What is Property?" "All property is theft" was his equally famous answer. If true it would follow that property, like any other instance of theft, marks a breakdown in some essential, regulatory social relation. This seems right: one taproot of our ecological problems is our quaint, historically provincial idea that we can have property in land, that we can own nature, that we can claim for ourselves sole possession and the prerogative of control over something so intimately connected to everything else in the world, everything that reaches beyond us, everything that might once have taught us humility and limit and a sense of our own place. All property is narcissistic.

And yet now I am a property owner, the co-owner of this pond which our lawyer, at the closing, ominously called an attractive nuisance. And attractive it is: after our first week in the house someone sends us a postcard with a picture of our waterfall on it. People stop to photograph each other in front of it. Amiably, I quit my lawn chores one day to shoot the breeze with a pair of cyclists and to take a pair of joint remembrances for them, one for each camera. I feel less amiable toward the camperful of teens who descend on the pond one warm day when nobody's home, treating our land like a public park. (Home from work to face a moral quandary: Do I chase them off? What do I say? Nothing in my ethic prepared me for that moment—a property owner skeptical of owning property, a theoretical communard interested very practically in privacy, in peace and quiet.) And the pond even attracts people when it's dry, as the traffic of passers-by and neighbors-to-be demonstrates.

The lawyer at closing, on a finer point of law: "You own the pond but not the flow, the thing the water makes but not the water in it."

Once as I worked on the dam I was startled by a whirring sound above me. Three feet above my head, ignorant of my presence behind the stone, a great blue heron was pitching in to land. If it saw me, it must have been too late to change its glide. Down it came, landed, and stood quietly in the mud, eyeing me. According to the law of entropy—the law whose depredations I was resisting by parging and striking, repairing my dam—this heron (any animal, any live thing) is a brief incorporation of energy, a momentary pool in energy's inevitable flow from higher to lower states, a bit of solar power and soil turned to food turned to feathers and wing and whirr.

In the grand scheme of things the heron may be temporary but what it represents can't be said to be precarious. Life thrives in the boggy pockets, the cool pools and the marshy meanders of energy's downward flow. Entropy doesn't mandate a linear, smooth descent from higher to lower states, can't prevent life from colonizing the flow, seizing it, making it stable at some level above absolute zero, just as my dam captures Pekin Brook to make a pond higher than Lake Champlain, the St. Lawrence, sea level. If my dam didn't have a bottom gate I would have discovered just how much work is needed to do the eventually inevitable, to lift that pond up over its confining threshold and release it on its way. Activation energy, the chemist calls it—the increment of energy that needs to be added, like a match to kindling, in order to move a system from an energetically stable state up over the rim and on a downward slide.

Fieldstone parged with mortar isn't exactly stable. Clay, I realized much later, after I was done, would have been better. The stones move a bit in winter, shift here and there from frost and ice. Clay would be flexible, would move and give with them, with time.

Next time, I think.

Once during a game in midseason T.Q., our shortstop, went deep in the hole for a ball, came up with it, wheeled and cocked his arm, and let fly to first. T.Q. was maybe thirty-one, had maybe been feeling in that summer the first twinges of his youth leaving him, maybe feeling other pains and pressures. Uncharacteristically he had fought with an umpire two nights before and been thrown out of a game. Softball had never been that important to him. This ball sailed up, over the first baseman's head, stayed up over the fence that bounds the playing field, a rifle shot whose next contact with earthly objects was its denting of a fender in the parking lot. Thunk! T.Q. threw down his mitt and walked off the field and never played softball again.

Maybe there's something admirable in such clarity, such obstinate dedication to ideal. But more and more it seems to me that what took T.Q. out of the game was a sorry, misguided absolutism—the same quality of mind that leads other people to anticipate apocalypse, or to long for a supposedly simpler past, or to straighten out a meandering, "inefficient" streambed, or to abandon in any one of a thousand ways a world (*this* world, with its temporal passages and trepidating change, its fickle weather and near-infinite press of equivocating particulars) for whatever hermetic solace they can find, wherever they can find it: at the mall, in the platonic ideal of the cosmopolis, in the gauzy embrace of nostalgia, in the silence of a virgin wood.

In the bar league we play at night under lights, down by the sewage treatment plant, a circumstance distinctly short of ideal. The first two years our team was together we played in daylight, to no schedule, pickup games against haphazardly organized teams from other bars, other towns. But such informality, however idyllic, required too much work, too much telephoning. Our schedule has freed us, but there is no costless benefit. Some nights the sewage plant reeks. Even when it doesn't, softball at night is a degraded thing, hardly comparable to those summer afternoons on former hayfields, on village diamonds tucked into rare flatnesses, fields from which I could see mountains, trees, high clouds against an azure postcard sky.

Softball, in the heat of afternoon, when the game is meant to be played: that is a memory worth storing. The regular change of innings, the fielders running to the field, the feeling we had playing a game tied to no clock, knowing as every player does *if the score gets tied, the game could last forever,* fanning out to our positions, running with the pleasure of physical effort, a chance to run in a game where running is usually brief, constricted, never social. With my aging eyes it gets harder and harder to see into the plate from right, nothing that would show in an eye doctor's test but a small, unmistakable loss in resolution, the result of life's thousand tiny corneal scratches. I ignore the waft from the sewage treatment plant and squint in to home, through the haloing glare of lights not high enough off the field, trying to pick up the ball the instant it leaves the bat, before it rises into the lights. I try to read its arc and distance in that first moment the way Willie Mays used to, when he would hear the crack of the bat and be running, not even looking at the ball but running for all he was worth away from home toward the fence toward the spot where cause and effect say the ball must come down, must be caught, and the ball would arrive there just as his mitt, upthrust, arrived to receive it. Physics, yes, and grace.

We all want to be Willie Mays. How many years since I turned my back on a ball?

The lights not high enough: the field, part of the Dog River flood plain outside of town, is a sandy soil subject to compaction, as hard as artificial turf in the drought of August yet easily penetrated by light poles, whose weight carries them down each year, incrementally down when mud season loosens the soil. Our memorial badge for Jeff (left center field, now deceased) hangs at eye level, though once it was way above us, higher than anyone could reach.

By day I parge my dam. By night I play in the playoffs, where I can't seem to engage my memory, can't keep hitters in mind from one game to another, from one inning to the next.

In winter I'll have conversations in town with men I've played against, men who assume that (a) I remember them and (b) I can speak intelligently about our team's experience this season, about our joint experiences, games we've played in against each other. I can do neither. I barely keep track of the score during a game (less to more; three runs up, four runs down) and often need to be told when our seven-inning games are about to be over. My memory is a sieve to this flow. I want the experience whole, not parceled into time-chunks with names and meanings, not dammed into this or that pool of experience. I want to immerse myself up to my eyes, want to drink it in without the intervening distraction of gulps, want to feel it course its way through me. One out, two outs, three outs. Back in to bat. On deck, batter up, ball, strike, ball. Over and over, a rhythm that comforts. Hermetic, yes, but a bounded hermetic world: a game, only a game, not life, not even close.

"What's your record?" the guy at the cash machine wanted to know. Lucky for me he's in a work uniform, a parts department, somewhere they need to see on his breast the name Buck. Dunno, I have to tell him. We're doing better this year than last. I think. Eleven-six? Eleven-seven?

A human being, I could tell him, is a kind of torus, an in-folded hollow tube, a ring like a doughnut, only longer, longer in the hole. We take in food, absorb what we need, pass on the rest. This is what I do with softball.

And the fieldstone dam, my dam, my thunderstorm dam—when I'm done parging, I reassemble the planking, tongues in grooves, and watch the dam collect. It takes hours to fill, much longer than it took to drain. There are still leaks, but it holds enough water to swim in, enough water to have a waterfall.

My dam holds back the flow, for now.

Ecology and Guilt

ccording to a brief and widely published wire story, on a cold January day in 1991 in the suburban precincts of Holyoke, Massachusetts, irate residents chased garbage trucks down the street, shouting epithets at the drivers, demanding that they stop. Other citizens, aware of what the drivers had done, called the Department of Public Works to complain. "The regional director of the state Department of Environmental Protection," the Associated Press reported, "threatened to repossess the city's recycling trucks and cancel its recycling program." What had got everyone worked up was the expedient by which Holyoke's Department of Public Works attempted to deal with the annual burden of holiday trash. Faced with chronic route delays and falling further and further behind schedule, drivers had been instructed to collect everything they found at the curb and throw it on the truck. The problem: "everything" included recyclable materials that householders had carefully separated into two categories (glass, cans, and metals; paper, magazines, and cardboard) and put alongside their garbage.

Standard practice in Holyoke has two kinds of trucks making rounds: regular garbage trucks and new, state-funded recyclables trucks with separate bins for the two categories. But, on that January morning, chronic undercapitalization caught up with the city.

"We needed three recycling trucks, and the state only gave us two," the public works superintendent, Bill Fuqua, explained. "It took five days to do three days' collections." The system was further strained by the holidays. Faced with what he saw as an unacceptable buildup of recyclable materials along the city's streets, Fuqua gave the order to the refuse trucks: "Take everything on the curb."

Fuqua hadn't anticipated trouble. He had made his judgment on clear cost-benefit criteria. "We felt," he told me, "that this was the most acceptable alternative. We looked at all the alternatives, more acceptable to least acceptable, and made a choice, how to deal with inadequate service." The amount of material, after all, was minuscule, compared with the overall burden of garbage. Trucks that day collected eight or so tons of recyclables, a small fraction added to the 12,000 tons of refuse that the city collects annually. And it wasn't as if glass and metal and paper hadn't ever gone to the dump. Recycling was a recent phenomenon in Holyoke. Routes were still being established, patterns still in flux. And, Fuqua added, the AP story was wrong in its particulars and exaggerated in its effect: the phone "rang off the hook," as the AP reported, not because of the unsegregated collection of recyclables but because of the delayed pickups that led to the collection of recyclables by trash trucks in the first place. By Fuqua's account, one resident came running after a truck, then called the Department of Environmental Protection— and the newspapers. The whole thing had been overblown and was, in any event, all over: the collection problem had since been solved through biweekly pickup of recyclables.

Still, those who saw the Associated Press story remember it. The incident gained a currency all out of proportion to the environmental damage that was inflicted or to the accuracy with which it was reported. I think the image of angry recyclers chasing garbage trucks sticks with us because it captures the truth that recycling programs operate not just in the realm of rational city management but also, and perhaps primarily, in the realm of moral symbolism. The irate response that Fuqua got was motivated not by a sense of wasted effort (though clearly if you separate things for recycling and then someone mixes them back together, that someone has just decided that you have wasted your time), and not simply by a sense of violation (though there's room for this element, too: the refuse of the self defines the not-self and thereby embodies a kind of negative of the self, giving the self a continuing interest in the disposition of the refuse) but by something deeper. Recycling has become the primary ritual activity by which we affirm our moral value against the difficult and unforgiving commandments of ecology. It's how we prove ourselves worthy of ecological grace, it's how we redeem ourselves, it's how we assuage our environmental guilt.

Recycling is, fairly clearly, the least you can do to reduce your negative effect on the environment. To have the least you can do undone by the act of another is traumatic. The image of citizens chasing garbage trucks figures an important truth: in ecological matters our sense of moral worth depends on the actions of others, and when you get right down to it we are all relatively powerless, post hoc petitioners of the machine, left to fume and sputter in its wake. You don't need to get mystical or structural-functionalist about the power that inheres in (and the taboos that surround the disposition of) refuse to see that by commingling what had been ritually separated the garbage collectors were violating profound conventions. Not only were they mixing the sacred with the profane; they were, in effect, condemning the residents they served to a kind of perdition.

Since Earth Day One many of us have struggled to reenvision our relationship to nature as a moral relationship. As more and more of us have found ways to do this, it has become clearer to us that ecology as a moral vision entails a rigorous and unforgiving ethic. Never codified, flexible because open to individual perception and yet severe for being ambitious in scope and minutely regulatory in detail, the canons of this system are the ethical structure that shapes our days. "Paper or plastic?" is a moral choice, not a lifestyle preference, and the Omniscient Moral Accountant watches what we do with every bit of orange peel, every sodden gob of coffee grounds, to see if we compost (building the soil: a moral plus) or simply trash them (a further strain on the solid waste management capacities of the watershed, an ecological demerit).

Ecology offers as an article of faith an absolute good, a good that true believers cannot be permitted to compromise: the continued health of ecosystems. As Aldo Leopold put it in *A Sand County Almanac,* "A thing is right when it tends to preserve the integrity, stability, and beauty of the biotic community. It is wrong when it tends otherwise." Like any young belief system, ecology is intolerant of dissent about the worth of its central value. Healthy ecosystems are necessary and right, and a morality in service to them is therefore objectively true, universally good, historically necessary. And, as with sinners in the eye of an all-seeing God, there can be no fudging of result, no escaping judgment. The integrity of the biotic community is absolutely beyond being influenced by what we feel, want, wish, or say. It is affected by what we do, and there's no way to lie or pretend about that.

These qualities of ecology as a moral vision threaten the line the western tradition has historically drawn between religion and politics. That line was intended to keep religious difference from spilling over into political difference. It separates revealed, absolute, uncompromisable truths about spiritual matters, on the one side, from a realm of conditional, evolving, perhaps imperfectly perceived (and hence negotiable) truths about the effective management of the polity, on the other. The line is more obvious in theory than in fact. It depends on the precarious and ultimately dubious distinction (drawn by Machiavelli, Hobbes, and Locke, reinforced by Hume, Madison, and others) between religion as an essentially private belief system of limited public moment and politics as a morally neutral, essentially technical pursuit of the public interest (which is usually understood to be the conquest of nature).

But the distinction between private morality and public politics is more mythical than practical, more hopeful than real. If moral life were simply a matter of right belief, the solitary individual would be the effective unit of moral analysis—the only entity one need talk about in discussing right and wrong. But moral life requires not just right belief but right action, and action takes place outside the self, and human selves are inherently social. The community, too, is a factor in moral matters. The political realm has always been one important arena in which the moral life of a community is articulated, symbolized, and transmitted. And despite the advice and admonishment of Enlightenment philosophers who tried to reduce morality to technical questions about long-range, appropriately enlightened self-interest, humans (even western "enlightened" humans) continue to think and to speak about their moral life in terms and categories intimately tied to the beliefs they hold most deeply as matters of faith and which are not merely private in scope.

Ecology takes this historically blurry line and makes it fainter. The hallmark of ecology as a politically relevant belief system is that it is manifestly not simply private, not simply "what one chooses to believe for oneself." It is a set of perceptions and prescriptions that are of necessity global in the scope of their claims. If I alone among two hundred and fifty million Americans recycle, I will still drown under mountains of trash and suffer the environmental consequences of our rapacious use of resources. My ethic requires me to try to change the behavior of others. If recycling does not become a public ethos, I fail in my ethical and practical purposes.

Similarly, while ecology honors the need for diversity of cultures (and would, if it were our regnant morality, do more to protect that diversity, since unecological economic development is the main force homogenizing the world's cultures into a world culture), it is ultimately no friend of the cultural relativism that says different cultural practices, different paradigms, are equally valid. If I am morally compelled to refrain from exterminating a species, so too must humans in other cultures be restrained. Their extermination of that species kills it just as dead and would deny not just them but me, too, the experience of it. My ecological ethic thus advances a claim to control their behavior, no matter that their hunting or farming or rain forest clear-cutting practices are consistent with an integrated belief system that (I'm willing to grant) has the same legitimacy for them that mine has for me. Because ecology suggests values that are by their nature global and absolute, it is as difficult to encompass within the political sphere as any fundamental, proselytizing religion.

There are other parallels between religious and ecological belief. In *Moral Man and Immoral Society,* Reinhold Niebuhr catalogs the characteristics of what he calls "vital religion" (a religion still expanding, still energetic, still growing), and it's a simple matter to run down the list and see that each has its application to ecological belief. A vital religion offers a millennial hope. It views history as the soul writ large, as the scene of a struggle between good and evil. It is "as impatient with the compromises, relativities and imperfections of historic society as with the imperfections of individual life." Each—the forward-looking hope, the sense that history is a Manichean struggle, and the tendency to devalue what exists in the present because so far evil seems to be winning—has its parallel in ecological belief. A vital religion also tends to draw such a sharp contrast between what is and what might be that the believer is led to despair of achieving the ideal in mundane history. In response to that despair, vital religion offers consolation that grows not from an image of gradual and inevitable evolution toward the ideal but from the certainty of dramatic, discontinuous change—the certainty, in a word, of "catastrophe." (Niebuhr makes this point to show how Marxism functions as a vital religion. The communist revolution is its apocalypse, its redemptive catastrophe.) The parallel with ecology is obvious.

Then, too, ecology and religion are both "fruitful of the spirit of contrition"—a believer in either "is filled with a sense of shame for the impertinence of [their] self-centered life." The sinner's shame in the eyes of an omniscient, judgmental God has its parallel in the ecology-minded citizen's dismay at their unavoidable participation in an unecological economy. As proselytizing, activist belief systems, ecology and vital religions both require "at one and the same time humility before the absolute and self-assertion in terms of the absolute"—that is, they require that the believer be humble before their God, but not so humble that they don't believe that they, as believers, are morally superior to nonbelievers. And in a vital religion, the enormous distance between the holiness of God and the wretched sinfulness of humans indicts humans not for particular offenses against morality but for a condition more complete than that: believers are guilty of being human rather than divine. Similarly ecology as moral vision charges us not with particular offenses against nature (or, not these alone) but with a condition more comprehensive, more essential, more unanswerable. By its lights we fail to be holy; we fail to be Natural.

In either sort of belief system the quest for the ideal leads, naturally enough, away from corrupt society. Thus, a recent letter-writer to the editor of *Earth First! The Radical Environmental Journal* bemoaned the fact that "being part of this society demands endless and constant compromises of my environmental ethics. Every time I use electricity, flush the toilet, or get in the car, I am knowingly contributing to the degradation of the environment." She announced her asocial intent: "I want to stop compromising. . . . I want to form a small hunter-gatherer tribe, which will use only the resources within its range," a group of "between ten and twenty men and women of various backgrounds and ages" who would try to live "authentically 'in place,' as humans did for 99.99 percent of our history." Which demonstrates that in ecology as in religion, zeal untempered by sociability manifests as individual, ascetic discipline.

Niebuhr sees too clearly the moral value of society, of a life lived in relation to others, to celebrate the ascetic hermit as an ideal worthy of emulation. And it is admittedly difficult to imagine humans shifting en masse to the livelihood of nomadic, preindustrial hunters. Yet, Niebuhr says, if asceticism is completely absent, that's "a proof of a lack of vitality in religion. A sun warm enough to ripen the fruits of the garden must make some fruits overripe."

There's no danger that the light of ecological precepts will fail to ripen fruit. If anything, the danger is the opposite one. The standards of ecological morality have clear and debilitating psychic consequences, consequences metaphorically akin to withering under a harsh, immoderate sun. On the newly moralized ground of our relationship to nature, our guilt is infinite and our means of expunging it both limited and dependent on the cooperation of others. This is obviously a formula for psychic damage: infinite responsibility, limited efficacy. When one of those others upon whom we depend for our sense of redemption fails to act in the expected ways—when the truck driver commingles what we, in good faith, have ritually separated—our response is not likely to be a reasonable discussion of costs and benefits. Our reaction is likely to reflect our sense that the very core values of the self have been threatened.

Our guilt is infinite because we are so numerous: in place after place, ecosystem after ecosystem, we have exceeded or threatened to exceed the margins of the planet's resilience, and thus almost every action we take contributes to the degradation of our environment. Given the overwhelming likelihood of global warming, every calorie of hydrocarbon fuel we consume is an offense against nature, against the extrahuman integrity of its relations. There is a law here, a natural law, relentless in its application, and we know it even as we break it: we ought to live sustainably, ought to act so that the preconditions of our acts are not precluded by their consequences, ought to obey the Kantian imperative to act so that we could reasonably and consistently will that the maxim by which we act be made general for all humanity. But every stick of fuel I burn in my woodstove is burned beyond the Kantian pale. Every mile I drive is a mile driven in violation of the law. I am always and in nearly every daily matter guilty.

Our means of escaping such guilt are limited and dependent on others because we are a technologically dependent people, and technology has long served us as an ethical armor, distancing us from the effects of our actions, insulating us from direct knowledge of consequences. I turn on the kitchen light. I do not see the acid leaching from slag heaps outside the towns where the coal is mined that produces the electricity that makes my bulbs' filaments glow.

Political ecologists are notorious Luddites, and for good reason. Not only are many forms of technology directly harmful to the environment, but the path to individual responsibility for one's own ecological effect lies in rejecting the mechanisms that prevent our tracing that responsibility—and that foreclose, through their collective nature, the possibility of establishing individual innocence.

If we do finally overcome this distancing, if we do come to understand the long chains of causation that connect the light switch to the slag heap, the knowledge we gain is likely to be theoretical rather than practical, a matter of inference and deduction rather than direct observation. There are many virtues in understanding a thing logically rather than practically. Theory-driven knowledge is clear, coherent, undeniable, pure. It tends to be unalloyed by the contingencies and half-truths of experience. Unfortunately, these virtues may count as flaws if the task is to build an ethical system. Moral truths unalloyed by the contingencies and partial revelations and messy half-truths of experience can overwhelm. What's demonstrably true in theory and in general cannot easily be gainsaid by particular facts—even if the particular facts are those of a life as a well-meaning, ecologically minded, composting, recycling, direct-acting citizen of the biosphere. The knowledge that we are, ecologically speaking, miserable miscreants burrows so deep within our psyches, and is so complete and so completely bound up with our membership in the human race, that it becomes *species* guilt: a form of original sin.

And indeed, the biblical story of the original sin seems to have a certain ecological, mythical truth to it. Since our expulsion from the hunting-and-gathering idyll of the garden—an expulsion consequent on our development of knowledge—we have transgressed against the earth. The secular political ecologist might disagree with the biblical myth's implication that in preagricultural society we were premoral and so prehuman, but could believe right along with the Christian that what caused our expulsion from the garden was not sin as such but the particular combination of hubris and knowledge. This amalgam is the very definition of civilization as we know it, of city culture with its ambition to control nature and its pattern of what biologist Alfred Lotka called exosomatic evolution, an evolution not of our bodies but of our tools. Pride and technics combine to produce a morally tainted enterprise that infects all who partake of it.

Having been prepared by Christianity for the idea of original sin, we seem ready to honor its form with a new content, and if anything we've found a more solid, more certain ground on which to view each and every human as fallen. At the bar of ecological judgment even the Amish (who I personally think do about the best job this side of Neolithic culture of living in accord with the precepts of an implicit ecological Kantianism) are guilty: just by breathing, the Amish (as do we all) exhale carbon dioxide and so contribute to global warming. Such is the comprehensive reach of the City of Economy that what might have passed muster in the City of Ecology will not serve, not here and now, not at all. In the world as it is, history seems to have carried everyone right up to the edge of the planet's capacity to accommodate our abuse, and in the simple act of living as humans, we propel ourselves across that border. There is no innocence to be had, not anywhere.

Once, at the recycling center at Casella's Waste Management on Route 2 outside of Montpelier, as I was moving from station to station, depositing the materials I had conscientiously sorted at home according to all the distinctions I have learned are important—boxboard is not corrugated cardboard, #2 HDPE is not #6 HDPE plastic, milk jugs are not plastic soap jugs, newsprint is not glossy inserts or magazines, green is not brown is not clear glass—I was struck by the number of categories we have proliferated. I saw that my sense of moral self-worth depended on my mastery of them, on my ability and willingness to sort objects according to them. The historic irony was obvious. I half-expected the recycling employee who corrected my deposition of material (white boxboard is different from gray boxboard; they can't take the former) to wag a finger in my face and admonish, like some scholastic philosopher inform- ing a pupil of a relevant category he's overlooked, "*distinguo!*"

Attuned as I was to these religious parallels, for a time I thought that a good solution to the psychic burdens of ecology as a politi- cal theology would be an Ecology Pope: someone to head the com- plex moral economy that ecology suggests, someone to model the perfection to which we all aspire, someone to manage a host of ecological practitioners (garbage collectors-cum-priest-confessors) who would counsel, convert, and cajole the populace. An Ecology Pope could oversee the dispensation of guidance, advice, solomonic judgment, and (most important!) absolution. I thought that the les- son of the Holyoke Garbage Truck Incident was the importance of absolution and the shortcoming of any ethical system that makes no provision for it. Without something like an Ecology Pope, I thought, the ecological believer gets no information back from the moral milieu, no reassurance that the effort it takes to be even par- tially ecological is worth it. Would you join an ambitiously and minutely regulatory church, one that offers no rewards for effort, one that says that even if you succeed in obeying the many rules and regulations you are still irredeemably guilty, guilty without hope of reform or forgiveness? No. One wants one's efforts noticed, one's failures forgiven.

In the absence of such acknowledgment, the believer tends to stray from the path of righteousness or to become obsessively at- tached to symbolic actions, since in these alone is the value of the self affirmed. Without a legitimate, outside-the-sinning-self au- thority to provide periodic absolution, novitiates in the Church of Ecological Disgrace may well chase garbage trucks down suburban streets, screaming at them.

But an Ecology Pope, I decided, is a bad idea. Of course no one person could presume to articulate and symbolize an ecological ethic. Nor could a human ever convincingly presume to offer for- giveness on behalf of nature. And part of the appeal of ecology as a moral vision is its open, participatory, democratic character; why invent a bureaucracy to administer it? I have come to think that what we need is not an Ecology Pope but a transcendence of the condition that makes one seem needed, the condition that suggests the parallel between ecological awareness and original sin. And so I think not absolution but absolutism is the problem: we need to reconsider our tendency to see moral valuations only in terms of extremes, our tendency to sort our moral experience into rigorously defined and separated categories.

I think we need to commingle, like one of Superintendent Fuqua's truck drivers, what we in the American tradition have ritually separated: we need to mix "innocent" and "guilty" by cutting across the moral dimension of our experience along a new axis, a new line of cleavage.

The axis we want is suggested by an insight from John Stuart Mill, who in his classic *On Liberty* argued that we ought to tolerate all kinds of belief systems—even, he tells us, Christianity, which as practiced has specific shortcomings as a moral system. No fan of revelation as an epistemological strategy, antagonistic to religion in general, Mill is perfectly willing to enumerate those shortcomings. "Christian morality has all the character of a reaction," he wrote. "It is, in great part, a protest against paganism. Its ideal is negative rather than positive; passive rather than active; innocence rather than nobleness; abstinence from evil rather than energetic pursuit of good; in its precepts (as has been well said) 'thou shalt not' predominates unduly over 'thou shalt.'"

Innocence rather than *nobleness*. What has it cost us, over the centuries, to value the one rather than the other?

Mill doesn't take the time to note that Christianity as it is practiced is but one of many possible Christianities derivable from Jesus' life and work and that the Jesus of the parables seems very much interested in the energetic pursuit of good. He does allow that ideas and feelings not sanctioned by the passive, reactive character of Christianity have had a hand in shaping European culture, or otherwise "human affairs would have been in worse condition than they are now." He might have added, such ideas and feelings have had less play in America, much less. For better or worse, mainstream moral sentiment in our culture is overwhelmingly dedicated to the ideal of innocence. It is a grudging, retrograde, backward-looking ideal, supporting a reductionistic, absolutist, Manichean ethic. The ideal of innocence celebrates an a priori state of being rather than an a posteriori quality of character. You begin life in a state of perfect moral grace and can only go downhill from there. The qualities of character you might develop as you mature are largely irrelevant to your moral worth. As Nietzsche argued (some decades after Mill), the ideal of innocence is the foundation of a morality perfectly suited to victims, to the weak, the timid, and the powerless, a morality that never quite escaped its origin in a tribe under military occupation, a morality that appeals especially to those who (for whatever reason) have been held suspended, inefficacious, actionless, denied purpose in the world. It encourages sentimentality (and sentimentality's companion political emotion, resentment): the moral ideal it offers us is a Norman Rockwell child, pure in its milk-fed, freckled innocence and chaste in its preexperience ignorance. The Greek tragic hero leaves it unmoved or moved to rancorous pique. The hero's difficult knowledge seems irrelevant, his motives suspect, his fate deserved. Why this fuss and bother about the agony of his choices?

Since by its lights ignorance is blessed, the ideal of innocence helps account for the strain of anti-intellectualism that exists in American life. It's also the hidden root which, revealed, shows brutality and sentiment, hatred and schmaltz in their essential relation as complements. Wasn't Hitler sentimentally attached to myths of Aryan virtue, Aryan prerogative? And the antiabortion partisan, who can sentimentalize the fetus as an archetypally pure, helpless, innocent being (a preexperience, prefall, prelife life) can also endorse or otherwise "understand" the cold-blooded murder of a postbirth, postexperience, supposedly fallen abortion doctor. We've even shaped the story of America's creation into a myth of innocence, a story of political virgin birth. Aggrieved and ultimately victimized by British intransigence, we acted not on our own volition but in response, as victims, only as provoked, and so achieved a species of political grace.

More recently, the morality of innocence accounts for some part of the esteem in which American culture holds the ideal of youth and also for the persistent American belief that experience can be consumed without effect, that no act is irreversible, that life and time need not leave their mark upon us. So too we might detect the specter of this ideal in how this temporal narcissism of American culture is played out. As a people we suffer not (as the old saw has it) from an ignorance of history, or from lack of interest in its lessons for us, but from an excessive preoccupation with its moral meaning: individually and collectively we're always churning through our stories, transforming them in the light of new experience, reducing their hold on us by making of them impermanent, insubstantial works-in-progress. We do this not to correct the record in the light of new perspective or wisdom, or to wring from our experience the last bit of enlightenment it has to offer, but because our belief in innocence requires us to return continually to our past (where, presumably, we once were innocent) in order to demonstrate to ourselves and others how we arrived here, in the fallen present, through no culpable action of our own.

Is our foreign policy a strange mixture of generosity and vengeance? Do we frequently act the role of bully? If you want, you can blame, as George F. Kennan did, democracy and the democratic polity's similarity to a great beast, slow to arouse and difficult to stop or manage once in motion. But blame, too, the widespread acceptance in this democracy of the categories of the ideal of innocence, categories that encourage us to demonize those who willfully disagree. Saddam Hussein had his chance to align with us and didn't take it; therefore he is consummately evil. Our salvation depends on believing that the guilty do not go unpunished and that one does not compromise with the devil and remain innocent. We use violence, then, not for its utility in international relations (distasteful as even that use might be) but for less defensible reasons. We are belligerent out of a deep-seated psychic need—which is to say, we behave the bully.

The categories of the ideal of innocence are also visible in two millennia's worth of our western notions of sexuality, where they held that an unmarried woman could only be madonna or whore, virginal or fallen. (Once fallen a woman was frequently rightless, prey to any man's desire; innocence being absolute, she could not be further violated.) Similarly, the ideal of innocence lurks behind some of our most influential and wrongheaded American attitudes toward nature: an ecosystem is either pristine (virginal, "natural") or tainted and not worth preserving, redeemable only through being turned to productive use. It's fair to see it, too, behind contemporary debates over the politics of gender relations and political correctness. In these latter cases especially it prevents progress, and ironically so: people who belong to groups that have historically been victimized now wield as weapon an idea, the Manichean division of the world into innocent "us" and guilty "them," which was once instrumental in effecting their own oppression. But this isn't so strange. Historically, peoples in search of liberation have tended to settle for a transvaluation of values within categories and rules they understand. They don't want the rules of the game changed just as they are starting to make progress under them. And, very clearly, victimized groups have made progress: under the existing rules of the morality of guilt and innocence, to demonstrate one's victimhood is to establish one's claim to the moral high ground.

The cult of victimhood is only the most obvious result of the way our valuation of innocence as a moral ideal leads people to try to construct their innocence—a project as corrupt and pathetic (and ultimately as futile) as anything ever done by the Army Corps of Engineers in their efforts to control the forces of nature. Properly, we may hope or petition for grace and hope that we recognize it when it comes, and we may try to live our lives as morally as we can, struggling to do right in each situation, and to do more: not just what is right but what is exemplary, what is in harmony with

the highest purposes and aspirations of the species as we understand these to be. But we cannot, not by lifting a finger or incant-
ing any combination of words, not even by demonstrating moral
wrongs done us by nameable others, ever recover anything of the
state of innocence that was ours, naturally and naively, before we
gained experience.

I think we shouldn't try. The efforts of those who do try tend
to be forced, pathetic, and (eventually) brutal. Often the attempt to
demonstrate one's own innocence is congruent with the attempt
to demonstrate the collective guilt of some other kind or category
of person. By far the largest portion of evil done in our world has
been done by people who understood themselves to be victims and
who felt themselves justified in perpetuating fresh injustice on some
group of guilty others.

Rather than feel guilt for our every breath, we need to acknowledge that humans who are a part of nature cannot be guilty for their
use of it.

I don't mean to suggest by this that any of us, individually or
collectively, has moral warrant for an ecologically oblivious life. I
don't mean to endorse the current cultural practice by which we
glut ourselves with commodities, asking only that they be shrouded
in a patina of green-pandering advertising. I don't mean to assuage
those shreds of guilt that might lead a person toward composting
and away from trashing by claiming that one can, after all, remain
noble while passively causing the world's resources to be churned
through for one's pleasure, comfort, amusement, distraction. No.
Humans who are a part of nature can't be guilty for their use of it,
but most of us are not, now, a part of nature. Were we to live and
breathe and think and feel in nature, we would have and spend a
great deal less. But it seems to me that guilt is part of the problem,
that guilt stands in the way of our recognizing our role and responsibility. It stands in the way of our effecting a reconciliation with
the planet. At a practical level, it's a strange person who'll join a
church that offers guilt but no prospect of redemption, and this I

think helps to account for the slow progress of ecological enlightenment since Earth Day One way back in 1971. At a more abstract level, the very idea of guilt presumes separateness, an over-apart-from-ness. This suggests that ecological guilt is the product of a too-clear division between people and nature, not a path to their reunion.

Maybe a sense of shame is what we want: shame signals connection, the introjected opprobrium of others whose good opinion we need and value. If we could truly feel shame in front of nature, shame in front of the needs and interests of other species, shame in front of an omniscient, all-experiencing Ecosystem, we would be constrained to live according to something like an appropriately environmental ethic. Far from requiring this, guilt doesn't require others at all, not even other humans. It can be keenly felt even in the most solipsistic of moral systems. Guilt stems from the violation of principle, not the violation of social mores, and so is more anonymous, more abstract in origin. That abstraction is a virtue when the community is unformed or unaware of itself as a community or when its regulating values aren't particularly enlightened. But when disconnection itself is the problem, a moral system that relies on guilt faces its limit.

An analogy: Shame is the wage of sin in a moral economy that trades, face to face, by barter. Guilt is the coin of moral exchange in a large and invisible market, where it, like money itself, facilitates the manipulation of the behavior of strangers at a distance. We think guilt is functional because as long as we remain a technological society we'll have a need to influence the behavior of individuals we never see, individuals displaced temporally and geographically from us and from the consequences of their actions, and law alone seems insufficient to the task. The rigidity of law is too constraining, and anyhow it's probably impossible to spell out in detail everything that should and shouldn't be permitted (though the tendency, over time, is to try). Instead, we'd rather just be able to assume good faith and good intentions. The concept of guilt helps informally to enforce that other-regard we seek.

But other-regard can be accomplished just as well within a moral economy of nobility.

In the moral economy of guilt, grace (or redemption, or salvation, or moral worth) is modeled on sexual virginity. It's an a priori quality of character that we all once had (though it's scarce among adults), it's an absolute with no partial states, it's easily alienable through the actions of others, and once lost it's difficult if not impossible to recover. Presenting us with its irreducible either/or, the moral economy of guilt is fundamentally antagonistic to the idea of gradation and development in time. It's antagonistic to nonapocalyptic change, to history. In contrast, the moral economy of nobility advances an a posteriori ideal of moral worth that fairly requires a historical sensibility. Its ideal is a moving, growing result, a result of one's own choices and behavior, a result whose character and scope are necessarily context-dependent rather than absolute, a result that can be cultivated as well as alienated, a result that, because it must grow and be exercised in experience, is not nearly so difficult to reconcile with life, action, and efficacy in the world (even in this imperfect world-as-it-is). A moral economy of guilt is a moral economy that celebrates childishness. Small wonder we perpetually seek to distract ourselves with toys. Within a moral economy of nobility we might learn to appreciate wisdom, might actually see a cultural turn away from the accumulation of things and toward the cultivation of understanding.

Just as in social matters we've got to get over the rigid dualism of guilt and innocence and think on a continuum of more or less noble, in environmental matters we've got to get over the romanticism that finds that *parts* of nature are innocent, *parts* are worth saving, *parts* have aesthetic appeal. We have to get over defining nature (and ourselves, our tribes, our groupings of people) in terms of sacred or profane, valuable or fallen, tainted or good.

In the western tradition we have long been accustomed to taking nature to be the measure of our ethics. As John Rodman has said, we have habitually justified our political systems by appealing to how (we perceive) things are done in nature. But history and circumstance have forced a reversal upon us. Our ethics are now the measure of nature, of what parts of it will and won't survive. Nature and ethics are like two shapes in a gestalt diagram. For millennia, nature was the large, imperturbable background to the foreground development of ethical systems. The ethical systems either referred to nature (if they were "naturalistic") or not, but in either case they comfortably assumed nature as the great, unaffected backdrop of our activities. Now that relationship is reversed. Nature is no longer outside culture, and our relationship to it is our single largest ethical problem. Our own history (imperfect and time-bound though our perception of it may be) is our likeliest source for a legitimizing, larger-than-the-sinning-self ethical authority. The litmus test of our ethics is and must be (as Aldo Leopold suggested in *A Sand County Almanac*) the historically minded question, Does this action, belief, behavior tend to promote the health and beauty and stability of natural systems, or not? An environmental ethic without a historical consciousness is inconceivable.

For millennia we have presumed on nature's good nature. We've expected her to provide for us, to forgive us, to indulge us our ill-considered and hurtful ways. But now culture has absorbed nature and we are the larger entity. It is time for us to reciprocate, to exhibit a generosity commensurate with our station. No more longing for babyish innocence, for the moral high ground of the powerless! We are not now that impotent, and the wish to be so is unseemly. It is time for us, as a species, to put away childish things and to accept our roles as part and partner of nature. We can begin by cultivating an ecological and historical understanding of our home range. Where does our water come from? Where does our sewage go? What soil feeds us? How was that soil built? What lived and died here a century ago?

With such rooted knowledge we must do what we can, and do it as well as we are able, and always strive to do more and to have others do more. In doing this we must not let ourselves be seduced by the ideal of innocence or be paralyzed by its converse, dread at the certainty of our guilt.

Why History Is Sublime

I was just about to work on my car—had just crawled under it, to assay the size of the bolts on the drive shaft—when Chris and Janet arrived with their one-year-old, Leah. Out I came, wiping my hands, smiling and waving. I never did get back underneath.

And so it is with dreams.

In my barn the engine stands on the floor with its own fluids pooling around it, staining the gray concrete, standing weirdly tall for being out of place. It's old metal and in design looks even older. Twenty-five years ago its British manufacturer sold romance and history, not modern engineering, and maybe that's why they went out of business. On a shelf to the left of the car stands a row of coffee cans full of nuts and bolts, each with its own masking-tape label, scrawled and telegraphic, neatly aligned with the others. They wait for me to empty them one by one as I reattach things under the hood, wait for me to restore their contents to meaning as part of this machine.

The car is a summer car, a two-seat convertible, impractical in this climate. It's an indulgence that I allowed myself, although there are so many other things on which to spend a tight underpaid teacher's budget. I feel a little guilty, owning it. Summers, I explain to friends, are short in Vermont. I don't explain that the car is part of my self's negotiation with parenthood, part of a promise to my-self that I am not old and staid, not yet. I do explain that I couldn't afford a car that didn't need a lot of work. When I am done rebuild-ing it, I'll reenact the ads I mooned over when I was fifteen, when I used to lie across my bed with my head hanging over the magazines and brochures on the floor, looking at the pictures until my head hurt from too much blood and I had imagined in every detail ex-actly what it would be like to own and drive a car such as this.

Where did I imagine I'd go? I can't remember. Destination was hardly the point. What mattered was motion and style, which I then was mistaking for freedom and purpose.

Between 1962, when the model was introduced, and 1981, when the factory in Abington was closed, Morris Garages made half a mil-lion model Bs, to a design that didn't vary much in the course of those nineteen years. "Changing, it rests," Heraclitus said. In this case the form, resting, changed. Sleek and sporty and fast when in-troduced, long before the last car rolled off the line it had become an anachronism, a crude, sluggish roadster easily outperformed by the boxy little sedans being assembled in Stuttgart and Yokohama.

Now one of those half million stands in my barn, without an en-gine, and another, engineless, with a body weakened by rust, is hid-den out back. (I speak of it as my car, singular, because the form of it, calling to me from its own future, seems obvious: out of two I will make one.) I had completely forgotten those brochures—had forgotten that once I wanted precisely *this* car—until, having bolted the driver's seat into the car, I slid behind the wheel and held it in my hands.

I had waited twenty years and I would have to wait one more. Chris and Janet's visit signals the end of summer, and with them arrives a knowledge I had hidden from myself: three days of faculty meetings start on Monday, and it would take more than a long weekend, even without company, for me to get the engine installed, wired, bolted, hosed, connected. When the semester starts I'll be too busy. The car will sit in my barn in pieces for the winter. I don't look back as I walk Chris and Janet and Leah up to the house.

Inside, I get Cheerios out of the cupboard for Leah and give them to her, dry, in a tin cup. My daughter is fascinated by Leah's babyish movements. She's ready to triangulate her position in time: Was I ever like that? she wants to know.

Chris and Janet are my wife's friends from another life, from before: when we lived in the city, when we were in college, when we were younger and childless. There is catching up to do. Over tea and coffee the conversation turns to the problem of God, the problem we all face as unchurched, more-or-less-agnostic parents. Do our children need a sense of ritual, the sense of comfort that faith can provide? Should we take them to church, even if we ourselves don't fully believe?

It is peculiar that we have this choice, though no one remarks on it. We muse aloud, tell stories really, and Chris and Janet agree that the answer is yes, even for us nonbelievers. I'm not so sure. Why gamble, I almost say, on your child's lack of imagination? Instead, I self-importantly give them advice. Most of the systematic cruelty that humans have done to each other, I tell them, has been done in the name of one god or another. Create new rituals, if you need them. Offer the child your faith, with all its qualifications and doubts. But steer clear of true believers, of revealed truth, of communities built on dogma.

Leah rattles her Cheerios, and then spills them; and soon our floor has little circles of dust on it, circles that owe their elements to the soils of Kansas and Nebraska, fine powdery circles that will dissipate, as we talk, under the tread of the children's feet.

Just before dusk I take the station wagon down to the village store for milk. Chris and Janet and Leah have gone, checked into a motel, after making plans for spending the day with us tomorrow. I leave Kathryn on the phone, long distance, to a friend in crisis. The friend wants to know should she live with this guy or not? Our child, tamed for the moment by television, sits cross-legged on the couch, bouncing a knee in silent distraction.

On impulse I go exploring on the way home: I turn up an unfamiliar road, the dead-end lane to the township cemetery. The way is overtopped with trees and under them the evening is thicker, dark and pungent like old oil. The lane's wheeltracks are deeply recessed and I creep along, worried about bashing the car's oil pan on a rock in the center hump. At the top of the hill I pass several ranks of marble tombstones, thin slabs stained by acids that rise from factory stacks half a continent away. Their messages are worn and indecipherable. They reinforce my sense that the position of cemetery commissioner, on which I vote every other year in the town hall, is largely honorary. The weigher of coal. The viewer of fences. The cemetery commission.

The lane turns to the left and rises into the open, where there is a diffuse and gentle lessening of the twilight. I can see that this is still an active cemetery. Here the stones are granite, the dates more recent. Some of the graves have flowers. Wendell Benedict, 1881–1962. Beatrice, His Beloved Wife, 1898–1962. The story is implicit, told quietly in stone by bare dates and names and an absence of signification. Did they die together? Or did she, his junior, succeed him in death? If she did: could she have meant to tell us about loneliness, about the power of love to command sacrifice?

A graveled turnout offers parking for a few cars and a view down the shallow valley. I park and wait. The cemetery commission has placed a trash receptacle here, a fifty-five gallon drum painted green. The mind registers the incongruity—what trash would mourners bring?—and then is calmed. The cans and bottles and plastic wrap are brought by others, adolescent couples mostly, who come for the view, for the privacy, to be alone with each other and their experimental approach to the difficult longings of adulthood. I get out of the car and stand in front of it, the better to feel the approach of night.

The day's humidity has gathered as haze, turning the Worcester Range a dark blue in the weakening, shadowless light. Below, behind the screen of trees, I can hear the cars begin their long sweep around the lake, past the gravel pit where on workdays dozers and bucket loaders remove the glacial till a truckload at a time. It's getting dark enough for the cars to have their lights on. Look down this valley: to the left and right the old, rounded mountains edge up into consciousness like dark stirrings from a dream you haven't troubled to remember. The evening light compresses distance, robbing everything of depth. The ridge lines seem thin, paper thin, layered and mounted like mica, each one darker than the one that lies before, as if the power of illumination had its origin somehow in the eye itself, as if to see, simply to see, were the difficult thing. There are taller mountains in the world, mountains made of younger rock, from whose heights one can see farther. But what they offer is spectacle, really, humbling vistas best left to prophets and adventurers and all the others who are enraptured by space or seduced by the heroic. Here the testament is different. The medium is time, the one dimension against which our machines must reveal their frailty. Endurance, these mountains tell us, is the larger power, larger even than transcendence, especially in a world unsure of its gods. This is why history is sublime. Against these mountains, all we do is small and human.

And here, alone, where the night will come soon to this, an open field with a crop of stones, next to a meager acre still in hay, I think: perhaps my life too will fetch up here. It is the township cemetery, and I have become a citizen of this town.

I could do worse, I decide. There is a good view, and a traffic of lovers, to commend it. And there is the road below, winding beside the stream that shaped this valley. It carries cars in a rush of motion and air and purpose, their passengers longing for their destinations, longing to achieve places I find great pleasure in imagining.